# CRUISING THE MAINE COAST
## MORTEN LUND

### WALKER AND COMPANY
### NEW YORK

Library of Congress Catalog Card Number: LC 67-13228

Published simultaneously in Canada by The Ryerson Press, Toronto.

Printed in the United States of America


The author wishes to thank W. W. Norton & Co., Inc.
for permission to quote from the following books:
*American Small Sailing Craft* by Howard Chapelle,
copyright 1951 by W. W. Norton and Co., Inc.
*Ranging the Maine Coast* by Alfred F. Loomis,
copyright 1939 by W. W. Norton & Co., Inc.
*Between Wind and Water* by Gerald Warner Brace,
copyright © 1966 by Gerald Warner Brace.

# CONTENTS

## AUTHOR'S PREFACE

This book, first of all, has a picture approach to the supremely picture-worthy splendors of the Maine coast. Those familiar with the coast who leaf through the book's many photographs will recognize, nostalgically, the captivating sensations engendered by this, the most ideal of coasts. And those who have never been to Maine's coast will herein be introduced to a new enchantment, that shoreline's clean and sweeping beauty.

This is also a practical book. It deals with the problems of space and time that meet the traveler by water on this coast. The book has a model cruise plan, embodied in a series of charts and courses distilled from the author's cruises in Maine. The charts are for the yachtsman's attention but they will be of interest to tourist and vacationer

alike. And then there is the body of the book, a log of my most recent cruise, spiced with some hints on the art of happy cruising in general, and a touch of historical background. It will enhance anyone's travel in Maine waters, whether armchair or actual.

We say "Down East" when we mean Maine. This is because, when you sail to Maine from any other state, you are commonly traveling north and east, running downwind with the prevailing westerly breezes behind you. You are, in other words, going downwind and heading east. This is "going Down East." The phrase has come to stand for the overwhelming, profound effect of peace and simplicity that the coast has on vacationer, yachtsman, and casual visitor. The words "Down East" have a magic to them, once you've been there.

*This book is dedicated to Pat*

## INTRODUCTION TO THE MAPS

The book contains seventeen maps. They are designed to show the main course (solid lines) and the side trips (dotted lines) of the model cruise around which the log of this book is written. Their function is also to show the relative positions of various main ports and harbors and anchorages at a glance: the large numbers with which ports, harbors and anchorages are marked will facilitate quick decisions underway. However, the maps are schematic and not intended as substitutes for the more detailed charts available through the Coast and Geodetic Survey which are on a much larger scale, easier to read in every last sounding and therefore alone suitable for navigation.

In sum, the maps in this book are designed to help you lay out overall course plans by vividly demonstrating the pertinent choices along any given stretch of the coast of Maine.

The first two maps are overall views of the coast from Kittery to the Canadian border. Map One shows the ten-day cruise East, setting a leisurely pace. Map Two shows the five-day passage West, leaving one day of a sixteen-day vacation to get from Kittery to home port. Between the two, the reader will have a good idea of just how much of the coast can be covered easily in a logical basic sixteen-day vacation along the coast of Maine.

### Maps

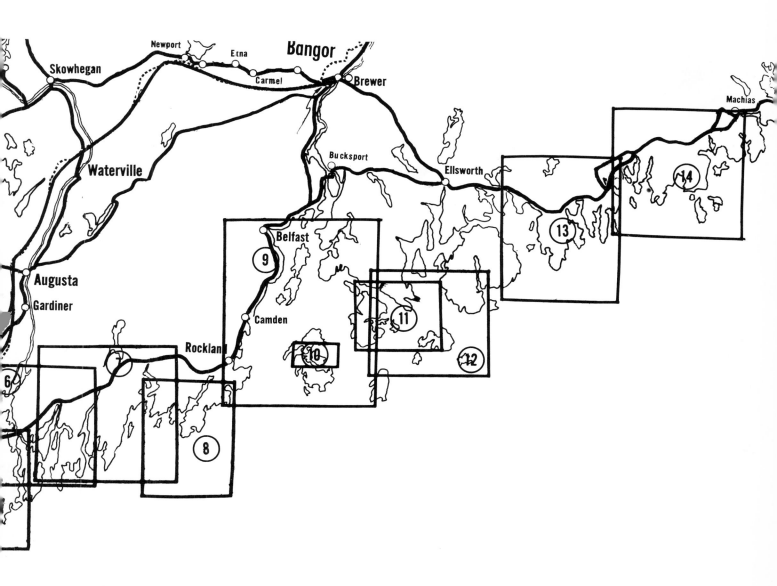

EVERY ONE OF my cruises to Maine has been a sudden, sharp confrontation. Maine's coast is a coast of startling, stunning, effortless perspective. There are a few people here, scattered in small villages up and down the tide line. But mostly, you are met head-on by the impact of long stretches of uninhabited rock and forest, of rock falling off into sea haze, of scattered insubstantial islets, of occasional white powerful plumes over a shoal, and a world whose stability is rapidly thinning away: a mere thread of land.

Reality turns out to be great blue shimmering sheets of water with no more than touches of land color here and there. And the very rarity and subtlety of these touches of Maine's color are her magic: the pale rose flush of her granite ledges, her lobster buoys as pin-pricks from a bright palette on a neutral ground. These are memories.

Maine has her dark tempers. Her weather can go slate gray in a few minutes and then her seas pour themselves on you in heaving hills. A whole world of fog rolls in and makes an instant mystery of the one corner you've salvaged. But the good days come. Then the sun floods a matchless sky and sea with unearthly clear light, small waves move flickeringly in ridges of shadow-blue, passing through pink and gray and bronze shores under the crests of dark and mint-green pines and firs. The rock islets glisten and the low cliffs run inshore for miles, framing blue ribbons of sea that disappear inward, compelling, inviting.

All this magnetic multiplicity draws the willing yachtsman on; it provides him with bewildering and bedazzling avenues wherever he may light: it puts him to many choices.

We can sketch a few of the coast's dimensions.

The *entire* Atlantic coast has a tidewater line five thousand miles long and of this roughly twenty-five hundred miles lies within the boundaries of Maine; the state's tide line delineates an incredibly convoluted coast, a coast turning in on itself like some ancient and patiently complicated Oriental design.

The need for intelligent selection in all this wealth is very great, if only because no one has unlimited time. Few of us have three full weeks to spend on the coast; for most, two weeks is probably average. It is doubly a shame, therefore, to waste a day in Maine. The road to happy and content exploration is a rational basis for picking good routes, given those two weeks. And a rationale is what I shall supply later: some further dimensions of the coast first.

Maine's coast is a "drowned land." Her coastal mountains long ago were sunk by the weight of the great prehistoric glaciers of the ice ages. They left Maine with a series of north-south channels making out from the coast and going back into the coast, channels formed by islets, islands, passages, reaches, and rocky shores. These were once valleys, ridges, and peaks of the mighty coastal range; now the range is a maze of fingered, split, sunk, and fractured rock at water level; the rock divides and shelters; the rock gives Maine's coast its unique and endearingly individual character.

And, most extraordinary: it all lies in an air distance of about 250 miles. This distance from Kittery, the most southern town to Eastport, the most northern town on the coast, is just about 250 land miles. Thus, almost any point on the coast is accessible from any other in a few days' running.

This accessibility makes Maine a lovely coast for the sail yacht. Cruising sailors today are not usually eager to set endurance records: the fourteen-hour, seventy-mile sail is something that they'd rather avoid, thanks. But a sailor can always get back out of Maine ("West'ard") in a hurry. For instance: he is due back in the office the day after tomorrow and here he is still east of Penobscot Bay. He can get to Portland airport in a day.

*Map 1:  Ten Days Down East*

*The map here is my "ideal cruise" along the Maine
coast, ten days going east and five days going
west. (See the return route on Map Two for the latter.)
The course shown is not intended to illustrate
the actual courses to be run, which differ greatly with
wind, weather, and time for each day's cruise
regardless of the optimum plan. But it is intended to
show that this coast can easily be divided into
short runs of twenty to twenty-five miles
each (four to six hours' running for a sailing
vessel) and still have each run terminate
at a place worth seeing.*
*Anchorages and harbors going East are as follows:
The start is at Kittery on the New Hampshire border.*

STOP 1: Cape Porpoise. *This is the first real Down
East harbor in Maine, well protected, with a
great lobster fleet and authentic Down East aromas.*

STOP 2: Peaks Island and Portland. *This is the
entrance to the famous Casco Bay and its myriad
islands. The anchorage at Peaks is well offshore; the
surrounding land is prime summer-vacation
country and year-round commuters live here as well.
Like the commuters, you can take the
Peaks Island ferry into Portland for supplies or sail your
yacht in to a float. Commercial Street, where you
come in, is one of the few really authentic harbor-front
cobblestone streets left on the East coast.*

STOP 3: Quahog Harbor. *At the end of threading a
suggested course through the fine, scattered islets
of Casco Bay, you anchor here in the calmest harbor of
them all in Casco, perfectly protected and
perfectly beautiful.*

STOP 4: East Boothbay and Christmas Cove. *East
Boothbay is a genuine small-town shipbuilding port where
the new version of the famous schooner America was*

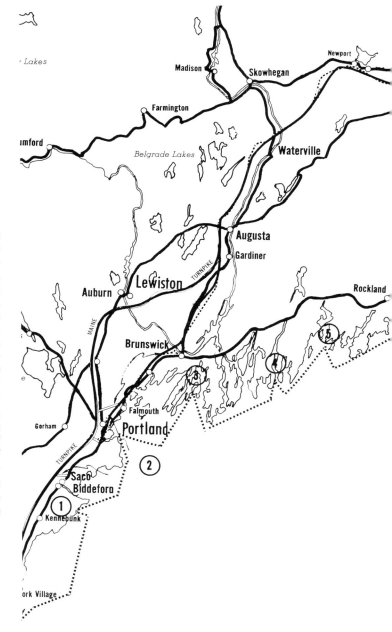

This is a planning aid; use only U.S. Geodetic charts for navigation.

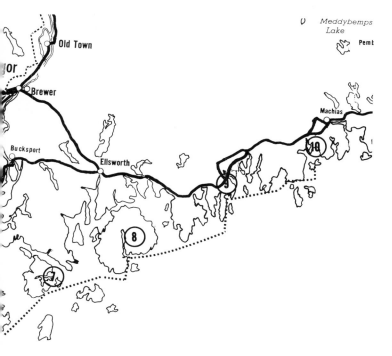

built. Christmas Cove nearby is a small,
secluded, select little summer resort.

STOP 5: Friendship and Otter Island. *The former is the
home port of the famous Friendship sloop
and the most "New England" of the towns of the middle
coast. The latter is a primitive anchorage not
far away on an uninhabited island; the water is deep, the
woods and beach all belong to the crew.*

STOP 6: The Basin and Crocketts Cove. *The Basin is
a landlocked anchorage on Vinalhaven Island,
connected to the sea only by a foaming tide run.
Deep-draft hulls prefer nearby Crockett's, a small
harbor offering nothing but peace.*

STOP 7: Merchants Row and Stonington. *Merchants
Row is a string of gemlike islands, granite
domes crowned with pine, set off the southern shore of
Deer Isle. Stonington is the "capital" of the island,
with plenty of supplies on hand and a main street full of
houses built when the granite quarries made men rich.*

STOP 8: Mount Desert. *The single most famous
location on the coast. Here are the famous high
mountains of the Mount Desert range, including
Cadillac Mountain, highest headland of our North Atlantic
coast; Somes Sound, the six-mile fjord where
Vikings once stopped over in the year 1000, lies in the
middle of the island.*

STOP 9: Pigeon Hill Bay. *This is a sail-through bay
formed by the island of Bois Bubert and the
mainland. The island is pleasant exploration: a freshwater
spring lies on one shore, and in the middle, a
freshwater pond suitable for swimming, to vary the
constant saltwater surroundings of any cruise.*

STOP 10: Roque Island. *This is a mile-long sand beach
enclosed in a huge interior harbor of the island,
considered the most beautiful anchorage in New England.*

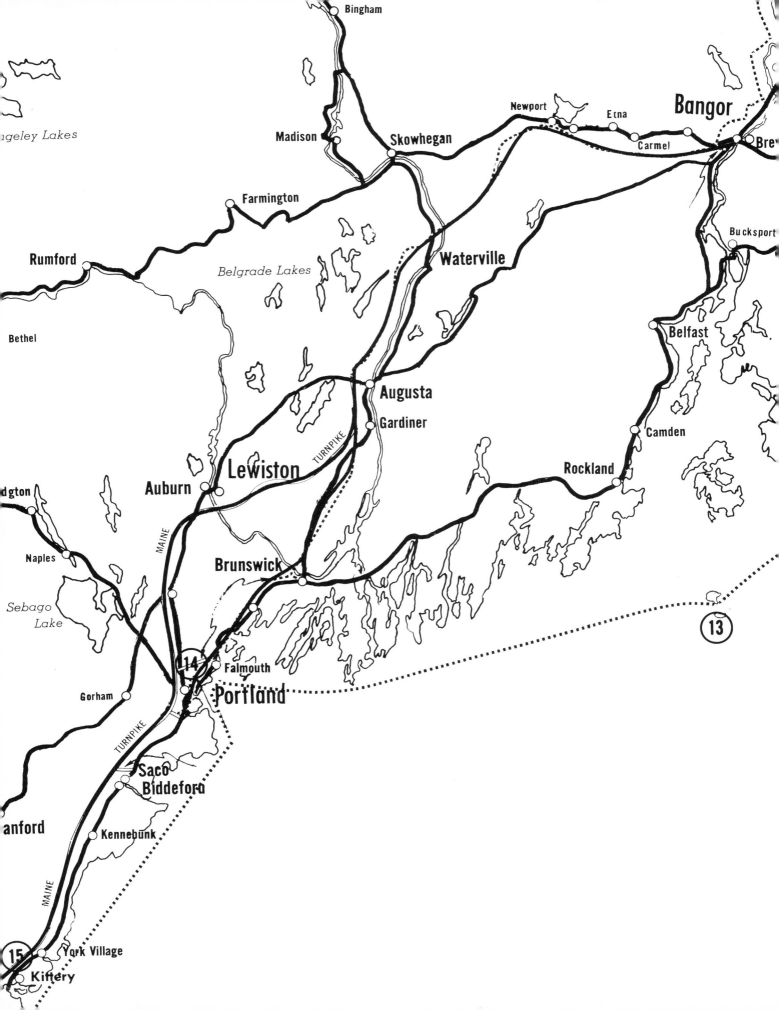

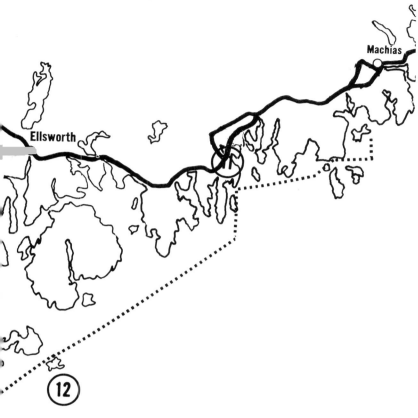

*Meddybe*
*Lake*

Machias

Ellsworth

(12)

*Map 2: Five Days West'ard*

*This map picks up where Map One left off: on the eleventh day of our hypothetical fifteen, we weigh anchor from Roque and head for Bois Bubert again. The course takes advantage of the offshore islands— Long Island, Matinicus and Monhegan—to get the crew back to the New Hampshire border in the fastest possible fashion without any letdown in the way of spectacular scenery and harbors.*

STOP 11: Pigeon Hill (Bois Bubert) and Carrying Place Cove. *On a pleasant day, the itinerary goes through Bois Bubert's straits again. For more protection and variety, it alternatively goes up into the next bay: Carrying Place Cove will hold off all but a hurricane once the yacht is hanging on its hook in the mouth of this long, explorable cove.*

STOP 12: Frenchboro, Lunts Harbor, Long Island. *This is one of the most storied as well as most isolated communities on the coast, and one of the last outposts of pure island living, with a magnificent harbor. The scene ashore is complete down to a seaside church.*

STOP 13: Matinicus and Ragged Island. *These two are the farthest offshore, inhabited islands on the coast of Maine, owning the best lobstering and the saltiest fishermen. If you want to travel back one century, this is the likeliest bet.*

STOP 14: Falmouth Foreside and Portland. *This is where you leave your charter yacht, or where you provision for the run across the border to New Hampshire; at Portland you can fly or bus to any New England town and to New York in a matter of hours.*

STOP 15: Kittery. *Then it's goodbye for another summer. But you'll be back.*

The coast is just as sweet cruising for the powerboat man. This is particularly true for the powerboater who does not calculate success in nautical miles. (The coast of Maine should be savored, not swallowed.) The powerboat man has multitudinous chances to fish, swim, clam, explore, sunbathe, talk to fishermen, find good eating places, and hike around on fascinating islands; he can afford to devote much more time to these things than the sailing man can. In this book I make no great distinction between power and sail in my "ideal cruise" plan. I simply assume that the powerboat man will get there first and have longer to enjoy it: the main stops are picked for enjoyment.

Maine's coast has been under the surveillance and care of men for such a long time that a cruise in Maine, inevitably, is a journey into the past, a stay among people who embody this past. The rhythm of the work of coast people, tied as it is to the rhythm of the sea, builds men and women of a character we have almost forgotten: like our ancestors, a people not easily perturbed by the peccadillos of man or nature.

Very early sagas record, and archeologists confirm, that there were Vikings along North America in the years around 1000 A.D. Leif Erikson ran here with his huge, low, square-sailed "dragon ship." If one interpretation of the sagas is correct, Leif's brother Thorvald lies buried in a Maine reach, dead of an Indian arrow.

The arrival of Columbus in the Caribbean was echoed in Maine. Hard on Columbus' heels, John Cabot coasted Maine in 1498. The Italian Verrazano came in 1524 and Humphrey Gilbert in 1583. In the early 1600s came John Smith, Henry Hudson, and Samuel de Champlain. Each of these left some record of their journeys in Maine. We can now fix their landfalls and encampments. Smith, for instance, set up a fish-curing company on the island of Monhegan.

The fantastic speed with which European fishing fleets reacted to the discovery of Maine has been

*At anchor, with Otter Island's*
*Harbor all to oneself*

*Modern hull and a classic hull, Buck Harbor*

somewhat played down in the history books. Gilbert, late in the 1500s, noted casually that he met over *thirty* fishing vessels from European nations along one stretch of the Maine coast. A bit later, one fisherman told Champlain that it was his forty-second trip to Maine (it was Champlain's first). Those fishermen were evidently great hands at getting to where the fish were, especially when there was a bounty such as existed in Maine waters in those days. And thus it is that fisheries, although changing in character, have been an unrecorded and yet sensible thread of continuity of the Maine coast through wars, blockade, famine, Indian siege, and economic disaster. Rockland fishermen still go out to the Newfoundland banks.

Maine lobster fishermen, who today make up the majority of the coast's seafolk, are not impressed with the exotic nature of their catch; they are fishermen for all that.

The solid establishment of annual fishing fleets in Maine at an early date unquestionably saved Plymouth, New England's first permanent colony. The several tons of fish given by a Maine fishing fleet to a Plymouth ship (it came north desperately looking for food) saw the Plymouth colony through that first winter. Otherwise the colony might easily have become —like Roanoke, Virginia, and Popham, Maine—only an historical footnote.

Maine has a special history for the sailor. Almost

of timber was perhaps England's greatest single reason for reluctance to grant independence to the Thirteen Colonies. England's power, bottomed in her navies, leaned a good deal on the pines of Maine.

By 1750, hundreds of ships were building in Maine at one time. Such was the activity that shipbuilding was the farmer's other source of income. Vessels built in a farmer's front yard were "swamped" to the nearest tidewater and floated to the sea. In the middle decades of the 1800s, Maine was hitting an annual pace of 200,000 tons of shipping a year. There were gundalows, barques, schooners, pinks, shallops, full ships and—greatest of all—the Maine Clipper ship, that glory-boat of the era of sail.

The ten thousand sailing ships were left to rot and now the wharves and yards are gone. And the hundreds of harbors where working sail once ruled are now inherited by the more delicate pleasure craft of the city-weary. The haunting beauty of this coast now belongs to those of us who sail for another need.

To fully encounter Maine along the sea, then you must anchor alone at times, as sailing men always have. And you must talk to the fishermen and develop a feel for the tempo of their life, for they live as our sailing forbears did. You must hunt clams and mussels along the shore even as the ships' crews did. From time to time you must claim parts of this coast by timely, if temporary, prior occupancy as the early fisherman under sail did. You will thus place yourself in the long chain of relationship that sailing men have had with this distinct and separate coast.

What is needed is the willingness to slow down a bit from your urban speed and get yourself aboard a yacht —be it big and brassy or small and simple, be it ocean-going or, just as happily, a half-cabin sloop, or be it a jaunty outboard cruiser. You can then enjoy the wild luxury of exploring, all by yourself, some of the finest, most history-laden and heartwarming natural seacoast that the world has to offer.

from the beginning, Maine was first and foremost dedicated to the building and maintenance of the sailing ship. At one time, her yards had built almost half the sailing ships flying the American flag. At the beginning, the colony's famous stands of pine were an extremely valuable source of masts for the Royal Navy. European mast timber had begun to be scarce. British "mast agents" were put ashore to keep the tallest timber safe for the fleet (the colonists cut them anyway) and the "King's broad arrow," a distinctive brand, was hammered into all timber more than twenty-three inches through the trunk. Just before the Revolution, Maine exported, in a single year, 382 masts, 69 bowsprits, and 451 spars to the British fleet. This supply

*Wind freshening on a rolling sea,*
*beginning of a blow*
*off the Western Coast*

HEREWITH BEGINS the log of our model Maine cruise.

Monday, August 8. Our first day at sea proved to be somewhat of a test. We had started off from Kittery on the Maine border in rolling, rollicking weather, with the long low line of Maine's western coast off to port, the lift and toss of the waves under us and the whole Atlantic to starboard. For several hours this was nectar for the soul. Here we had spread before us the prospect of abundant beauty, adventure, and peace. In these first hours' run for Cape Porpoise, our initial stop, we felt that tremendous surge of spirits that one gets when freed from the bondage of buildings, sidewalks, and stifling air.

We had a brand-new twenty-one-foot Grady-White Atlantic Weekender, an outboard cruiser with twin engines. The whole rig was handling beautifully. The swell would lift the stern and send us sliding down the face in a mild version of the surfboarder's ride for shore —except that here were ten thousand swells, each of them a ride. There is some skill involved, but not an extraordinary amount, in keeping a boat on course in such weather. For us, both a good many months away from the sea, this was just the fillip needed to kick the cruise off in style.

But by four o'clock there was a blazing thirty-knot wind gusting and the foam had begun to show in earnest on the top of gray moving rows of the sea. The hull, untried, was being twisted about, jolted, and dropped hard over toppling crests with ominous frequency. Would we be smart to keep on for Cape Porpoise? Or would we be better off hightailing it to the nearest shelter like a couple of schoolboys caught truant?

I looked quizzically at the crew, one Alan Baker, eminent Philadelphia bachelor, companion on a number of marvelous cruises. As we hung on in the cockpit, we could feel the jolts in our bones. Much more running in this kind of sea in a hull that hadn't had time

to swell properly might not make sense.

We checked to see if she had opened up. We lifted the floor hatches in the cabin and in the cockpit— frequently. No untoward amount of water was seeping into the bilge yet. And the twin 40-hp Evinrude outboard engines—also brand new—seemed content at half throttle.

By four thirty the crests had started breaking down from the watery ridge tops, trying to hit us broadside. Whenever we couldn't get the bow into them in time, we took a hell of a thrust, lurching about on the steep incline of the wave. Perforce, we were tacking: holding our course when we could and swinging to meet the runs of foam with the bow before they could give up trouble.

Now there was plenty of call for helmsmanship: the steep swells swerved us off to one side or the other as we came down from the crest; each swerve took the boat over onto her side a bit, so-called "broaching." (A "full broach" is one that turns a ship fully side-to the wave and rolls the ship over.) We knew that if you add an unlucky hit with a really big crest to a half-broach position, your yacht can easily find herself half full of water.

In all likelihood, the Grady-White could have ridden out the storm even if the engines had gone dead and we'd both been senseless in the bottom of the cockpit. The G-W is about as well-designed a seagoing hull as there is. But we were trying to make a definite harbor by a definite time. This means we were fighting the run of the seas and forcing our hull through the water. But drive her we did: we were not at all anxious to spend any part of the night off the coast.

At this point, Porpoise was still a good way off and I had some sharp second thoughts. Once we had chosen to start our trip at the very southern tip of Maine, we were stuck with a beach coast.

I do not like beach ports in rough weather. Getting

| Place | Height referred to datum of soundings (MLW) | | | |
|---|---|---|---|---|
| | Mean High Water | Mean Tide Level | Mean Low Water | Extreme Low Water |
| | feet | feet | feet | feet |
| Old Orchard Beach | 8.8 | 4.4 | 0.0 | −3.5 |
| Cape Porpoise | 8.7 | 4.3 | 0.0 | −3.5 |
| Portsmouth Harbor Light | 8.7 | 4.4 | 0.0 | −3.0 |

(863)

ABBREVIATIONS  (For complete list of Symbols and Abbreviations, see C. & G. S. Chart No. 1)

Lights (Lights are white unless otherwise indicated.):

| | | | |
|---|---|---|---|
| F. fixed | Mo. (A) morse code | OBSC. obscured | Rot. rotating |
| Fl. flashing | Occ. occulting | WHIS. whistle | SEC. sector |
| Qk. quick | Alt. alternating | DIA. diaphone | m. minutes |
| Gp. group | I. Qk. interrupted quick | M. nautical miles | sec. seconds |
| E. Int. equal interval | | | |

Buoys:

| | | | |
|---|---|---|---|
| T.B. temporary buoy | N. nun | B. black | Or. orange | W. white |
| C. can | S. spar | R. red | G. green | Y. yellow |

Bottom characteristics:

| | | | |
|---|---|---|---|
| Cl. clay | M. mud | hrd. hard | bk. black | gy. gray |
| Co. coral | Rk. rock | rky. rocky | br. brown | rd. red |
| G. gravel | S. sand | sft. soft | bu. blue | wh. white |
| Grs. grass | Sh. shells | stk. sticky | gn. green | yl. yellow |

21  Wreck, rock, obstruction, or shoal swept clear to the depth indicated.
(2)  Rocks that cover and uncover, with heights in feet above datum of soundings.

| | | |
|---|---|---|
| AERO. aeronautical | R. Bn. radiobeacon | C. G. Coast Guard station |
| Bn. daybeacon | R. TR. radio tower | D.F.S. distance finding station |

AUTH. authorized;  Obstr. obstruction;  P.A. position approximate;  E.D. existence doubtful.

HEIGHTS

Heights in feet above Mean High-Water.

AUTHORITIES

Hydrography and topography by the Coast and Geodetic Survey with additions and revisions from the Corps of Engineers and the Geological Survey.

STORM WARNINGS

The U. S. Weather Bureau displays storm warnings at the following approximate locations:
Cape Elizabeth Light (43°34' - 70°12')
Portland Lightship (43°31.5' - 70°05.5')
Fletchers Neck C. G. (43°26.5' - 70°20.5')
Portsmouth Harbor at Fort Pt. (43°04.3'-70°42.6')

CAUTION

Improved channels shown by broken lines are subject to shoaling, particularly at the edges.

CAUTION

Temporary defects in aids to navigation are not indicated on this chart except where a buoy replaces a fixed aid.   See Notice to Mariners.

AREA "1A"

Boundary limits of Submarine Operating Area "1A" are shown in solid magenta lines. As submarines may be operating in this area, vessels should proceed with caution. During torpedo practice firing, all vessels are cautioned to keep well clear of Naval Target Vessels flying a large red flag.

CABLE AND PIPELINE AREAS

The cable and pipeline areas that fall within the limits of charts Nos. 231, 211 and 212 are not repeated on this chart.

CAUTION

Mariners are warned to stay clear of the protective riprap surrounding navigational light structures shown thus:

*Map 3: Kittery to Wells*

The cruise begins at the New Hampshire border where the yacht can stop overnight at either the Islet of Shoals or up the Piscataqua River.

1. *Route from Isles of Shoals.* The route joins the main route (solid line) outside Kittery.

2. *Kittery Point. The first anchorage up the Piscataqua.*

3. *Kittery. The second anchorage is off the town of Kittery itself, lying on the Maine Turnpike bridge.*

4. *Portsmouth, opposite Kittery, is the gateway town to the whole large inland basin farther up the Piscataqua.*

5. *York River. A good alternate to the Piscataqua when entering Maine or needing shelter from storm.*

6. *Cape Neddick Harbor. Secondary shelter along the exposed initial portion of the cruise itinerary.*

7. *Ogunquit. Cheery tourist town with picturesque Perkins Cove; for social sailors in shallow-draft yachts.*

8. *Wells. Secondary shelter if you can't make it to Cape Porpoise by dark and don't like night sailing.*

9. *SLIDE course to Cape Porpoise (see Map Four, page 36).*

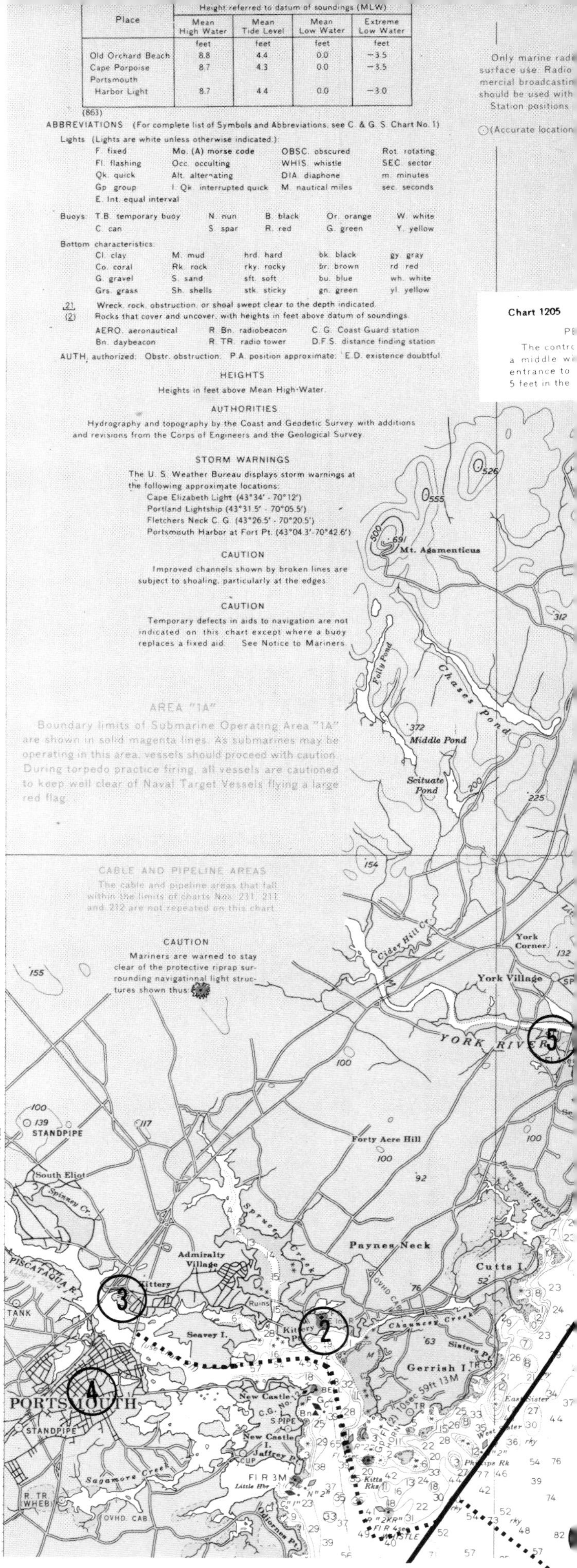

Chart 1205

This is a planning aid; use only U.S. Geodetic charts for navigation.

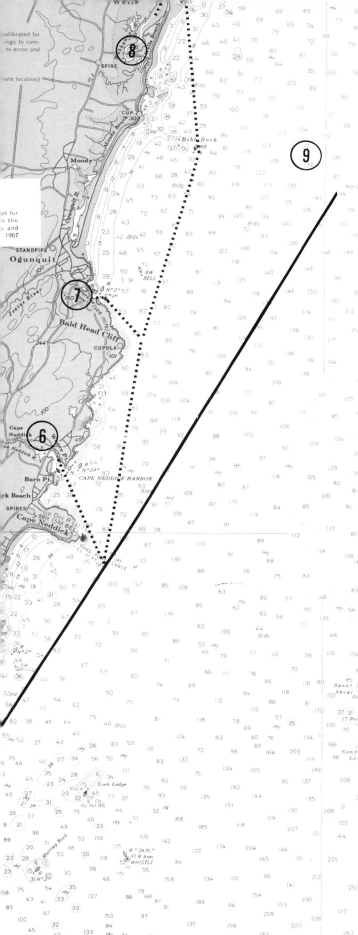

through a hole in a beach front necessitates running the surf. Unless you are used to this exercise, the sensation is hardly less than hair-raising.

On Cape Porpoise, luckily, there is no beach surf and the harbor lies deep. So we were forced to try for that port whether we thought the boat could take it or not. Damn the waves! Our dinghy, a creation of transparent Buturate by Sudbury Labs in Sudbury, Massachusetts, was dancing wildly about at the end of its tether and occasionally flying out of water like a cork out of a champagne flask, yanking as if the dinghy, too, wanted in.

We were taking a beating.

Another half hour of anxiety and we, although somewhat groggy, were within hailing distance of Red Bell 2 off the Cape Porpoise entrance. (See Map Four, page 36.) It was welcome. The wind obviously had no intention of slacking. In truth, it had that underlying feeling of vigor and willfulness which betokens a wind that is building. Our hull was now coming off the tops with a leap and then dropping with a heartrending crash on the downside. The gear aboard, which we hadn't had time to stow properly, was starting to come loose inside the cabin and was making ominous noises.

I was suddenly reminded of the last time I had experienced such a sea. It was a good number of years ago while I was on the staff of *Sports Illustrated* magazine. I was filling the job of crew for the yachting editor, Ezra Bowen, and our schooner was headed for a port on the Jersey shore. The schooner was a big one and there were just the two of us, so we were thoroughly shaken by the time we had rounded up and headed in toward the twin breakwaters of the harbor. The seas were running straight through the corridor formed by the breakwaters. Suddenly, one sea picked the schooner up bodily and *surfed* us; we rode the crest like Captain Ahab homing in on the White Whale. The schooner reached a speed which it had never—I am

*A sea beginning*
*to make off Cape Porpoise*
*with a fisherman nosing into it*

dead sure—reached before. As we rode in, we passed the Coast Guard station—we were still on our crest. I saw out of the corner of my eye that a complement of men had started to scramble for the launching ramp and some were loosening the ties of a rescue craft, just in case Captain Ezra lost it and slammed against one of the walls. But he didn't. We came whistling into the flat waters of the inner harbor with water creaming off the bow. We had momentum enough to circle the harbor once, looking for a mooring, without having to take the engine out of neutral.

The present situation was quite a bit better. Al Baker and I were in a boat with a good deal more power and maneuverability than a bulky schooner. And, equally fortunately, the entrance to Cape Porpoise, while not a snap, was a lot easier than the one on the Jersey coast. Even so, I had my work cut out at the helm to keep the hull trimmed. We went in with seas that were rising to new and greater heights as the waves rode into shallow water. Our approach forced us to make a sharp left inside the first marks; I made it as gently as possible and we scudded between the two ledges, aptly named Goat Island and Folly Island.

The whole approach was in what is known to be the thickest field of lobster-pot buoys in the world. Red and black beacons on the two ledges mark the inner "gate" to the harbor and in that strait the pots closed in on us like an improbable flotilla of multicolored Lilliputian men-of-war racing over heaving billows. It was almost impossible to miss them all, coming in with the seas behind us and having to keep a certain minimum speed to control the hull. I sweated out at least four thuds. If a pot line gets tangled severely enough in the props, you can have all kinds of merry hell in a situation like this one. Fortunately, the Evinrudes have slip clutches so that the propellers will not shear their pins (or cut the line) except from an extraordinarily unlucky blow. What you hear—what we did hear once

—constitutes an irritated whine when the slip clutch lets the motor rev until the prop pulls loose from the pot line.

And then we were in.

We relaxed tense muscles as our hull slid in among the boats of the fishing fleet bobbing in the calmer water. We circled a bit to get our bearings and then motored up to the gas dock (the town wharf on Bickford Island) to get some fuel on. The gas pier was a big platform set on high legs and we had to climb to get the attention of the dockmaster. We found, toward the rear of the dock, the water hose we needed. And we inhaled lobster-bait odors, a pungent smell which issued from forty barrels of not-too-well-preserved fish under an open shed roof at the rear of the wharf.

I forgive them all their bait. Lobster fisherman are, by and large, a very special and winsome lot. A prime example of what I mean occurred just here. We had climbed down and had left the gas dock; as we swung out we were crossed by a lobster fisherman who was helming his trim work hull past us. We asked if there were any moorings to be had in here. He pointed to an outer buoy and said that was his, and we could take it. He thus spared us the work of finding a space in which to anchor (anchoring requires more line and more room). We motored to the buoy indicated and picked up one end of the fisherman's mooring line. The other end was fastened securely to a heavy weight at the bottom of the harbor. We tied on and quickly zipped down the rear cockpit curtain (the clouds overhead looked ready to break). The rear curtains on the G-W formed a slanting awning which, when added to the side curtains, made a watertight and pleasingly snug, full-headroom, seagoing tent out of the cockpit. From our "tent," we hailed the lobster fisherman. We tried to get him to take a couple of dollars for his mooring but he waved us off. "How hard is it blowing out there now?" we shouted to him. "Forty," he shouted.

Full gale, in other words. Nice to be inside. It must be a real witch's brew out there now.

One of the great advantages of the powerboat over sail is that the enclosed cockpit of a power craft, when snugged with a good cover, has much more room to it than any similar arrangement can possibly provide on a sail yacht of remotely comparable size. On our twenty-one-footer, we had the kind of moving-around space in the cockpit that it would take a sixty- to seventy-foot sail yacht and a big doghouse or canvas awning to provide. In terms of money per inch of comfort aboard while at anchor (given a protected harbor), the motor yacht is far ahead. In bad weather on a sailboat, you are confined "below" off watch and somehow that is a great deal less satisfactory than be-

ing able to sit as we did, seeing ourselves swing at anchor, looking at the black-silver clouds move over the darkening sky, threatening to break, but not quite breaking, into thunder and rain.

Now the first thunderclap sounded from a threatening cloud and the sky was rapidly blacking out the small amount of evening light left. Rain started pattering down on the canvas, and then gusted down in wild polyrhythmic tattoo; we lit the cooking fires and the kerosene anchor light and soon the plastic windows of the side curtain shone out and lit the sheets of hurrying drops that slatted against us.

We downed a quick Scotch or two, neat. Shortly thereafter we did in the contents of two or three tins of food quickly brought to a simmer. The food—whatever it was—tasted like manna. Al sat back and fished up two excellent cigars from his kit and passed one to me. We lit up solemnly listening to the wet, thunderous hurly-burly.

I took a last peek into the hull's bilge. She was tight. And she'd handled herself like the superb design that she was. The Grady-White Atlantic Weekender is a sharp-bowed, wide-flare, plywood lapstrake (or clinker-built) hull and her performance of that day had proved the soundness of the conception. She had cut through the rough stuff; she had cushioned the shocks and stayed on her feet in spite of the fact that she floats very much on top of the water as all fast outboard hulls must. And now, as she lay nosing comfortably up and down in the slight surge, her tightly buttoned structure was ample proof against the wet and the wind. "Puff, the magic dragon, he lived by the sea," I hummed. I patted the hull affectionately. "Pass the Scotch."

"Good name," said Al, puffing away.

Flashes continued to turn on and off over the harbor, the sharp blue-white electrical light glared off the white sides of the lobster-fishing craft next to us. Shafts striking across the sky lit the cabin roof in flickering white. A big one came down ashore with a noise that shook the harbor, then lessening noise seemed to promise a calmer night ahead.

For the next hour or two I read and wrote. Settled under the kerosene lamp, checking my cruise itinerary, I fought with that feeling of uncertainty all planners have. Most cruise itineraries have two versions: the sharp Platonic ideal you plan and the somewhat fuzzied shadow of that ideal reflected on the screen of reality.

Ideally, our four-week cruise (consisting of a two-week basic model cruise plus some side trips) was to start off like this:

*August 8:* From Kittery on the New Hampshire

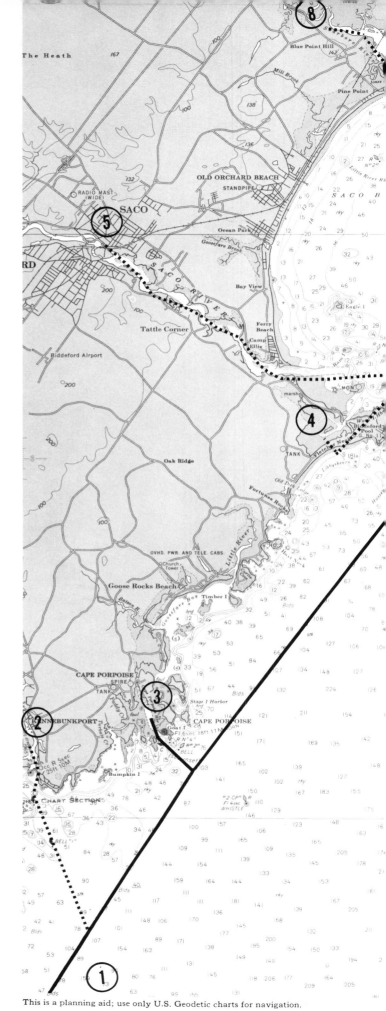

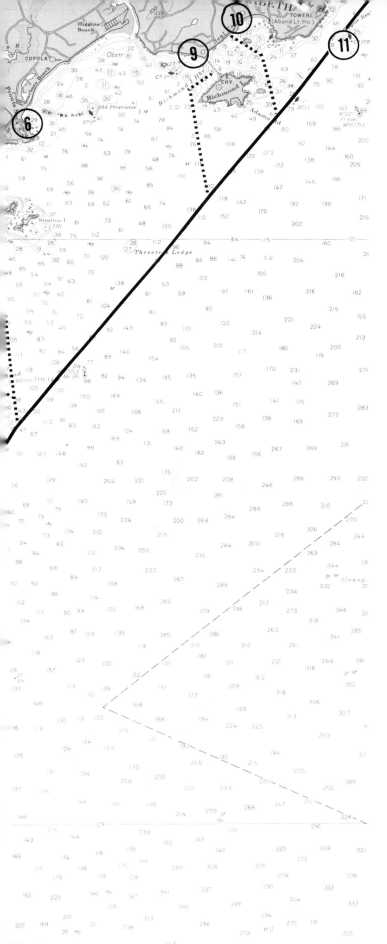

*Map 4: Kennebunkport to Cape Elizabeth*

The second section of the western coast of Maine takes the cruise to a point just below Portland and Casco Bay.

1. Course from Kittery and New Hampshire.

2. Kennebunkport. It's a bit hairy getting in here but it is a nice side trip if you have time.

3. Cape Porpoise. The saltiest of the western Maine harbors; STOP 1 on the course, and the usual first-night harbor coming into Maine. Beautifully protected.

4. Wood Island Harbor. Partially protected but interesting and not overfrequented. Biddeford Pool is the small town on the foreside.

5. Saco and Biddeford. Two industrial towns up the Saco River. No reason to go here except for emergencies requiring great shelter, doctors, or access to the Maine Turnpike.

6. Prout's Neck. Home of the famous Black Point Inn. Fairly open harbor but eating ashore is good.

7. Scarboro River. Affords more protection than Prout's Neck, depending on how deep your draft is.

8. Pine Point. A trip up here by dinghy will get you a few groceries if needed.

9. Richmond Harbor. Possible shelter from north and east winds.

10. Seal Cove. Protection from south and west if you have a good fathometer and steady nerves coming in.

11. To Peaks Island and Portland (see Map Five, page 64).

border to a main stop at Cape Porpoise, the biggest harbor south of Portland. We had done just that, happily.

*August 9:* From Cape Porpoise, on a side trip to Prout's Neck, the most sophisticated port south of Portland and the location of the famous Black Point Inn.

*August 10:* Prout's Neck to the main stop at Peaks Island and Portland (Maine's largest city), 60 miles from the start.

*August 11:* Portland to the main stop at Pinkham Point on the eastern side of Casco Bay plus exploration of Casco's myriad nearby islands and passages.

*August 12:* From Pinkham Point on a side trip to Augusta (the capital of Maine and the author's hometown) via the famed Kennebec River.

*August 13:* Layover at Augusta (on the beautiful Kennebec 'neath the walls of Fort Western).

*August 14:* Augusta to the main stop at East Boothbay (a really Down East small-town shipyard in operation).

*August 15:* From East Boothbay on a side trip to New Harbor (picture-postcard lobster-fishing port).

*August 16:* New Harbor to the main stop at Otter Island (typical out-of-the-way uninhabited small harbor or "gunkhole").

*August 17:* From Otter Island on a side trip to Camden for supplies.

*August 18:* From Camden on a side trip to Pulpit Harbor (most famous of the Penobscot Bay gunkholes).

*August 19:* From Pulpit Harbor to a main stop at The Basin (almost completely land-locked saltwater inland lake connected

by a tide fall to Penobscot Bay).

*August 20:* The Basin to a main stop at Winter Harbor (long, long stretch into Vinalhaven Island, granite-quarry country).

And so on. On Map One, page 20, one of the two overall charts of the "model two-week cruise," are listed all the main stops on the eleven-day cruise east. And on Map Two, page 22, are listed the five main stops on the five-day return cruise. The model cruise is set for sixteen days: two weeks plus a weekend.

The main hops are largely short legs of ten to twenty miles, suitable for a day's sail or motoring under a sail-

*A dusty southwester
taken in stride*

boat's auxiliary engine if there is no wind.

Inboards and outboards with much more speed, of course, could easily hopscotch about on this plan. They could skip the first stop and go on to the third stop or even the fifth stop, but my experience with powerboating (which includes the 800-mile Inland Passage from Seattle to Alaska) has led me to believe firmly in the true existence of "roar fatigue." I have concluded that you get roar fatigue after a couple of hours at full engine cruising speed, regardless of the hull size. This affliction dims your appreciation of everything around you, including the sensations of beauty and delight which were presumably the reason for taking the cruise in the first place. There is scientific evidence that your senses actually get somewhat out of whack when exposed too long to too much noise.

And then there is "wind fatigue." This is the sailing equivalent of the roar variety of tiredness.

You get wind fatigue less quickly on a sailboat than you develop roar fatigue on a motor yacht, true. But there still is an upper limit of four to five hours. After such an interval, you lose 90 percent of the ability to relax and enjoy the scene.

To sum up: I am against staging marathon marvels of helmsmanship down the shoreline, either by sail or power.

Nevertheless, in laying our cruise plan to reach Cape Porpoise at the close of our first day in Maine, our cruise cavalierly bypassed the initial twenty-five miles of the western coast of Maine. These are a mildly interesting twenty-five miles of the coast from a cruising point of view. But no one is going to say the westernmost twenty-five miles of Maine is *un*interesting and get away with it: only our decision to design a cruise that can be accomplished in a limited time justified our beeline to Cape Porpoise. There are *plenty* of things to see and do in the stretch from Kittery to Cape Porpoise.

*Seiners, starting to pull nets*

*A constant on the coast:*
*lobsterman's shack,*
*lobster pots and pot buoys*
*piled on a long-legged wharf*

To compensate the partisans of the western coast, the author intends to introduce forthwith in this chapter a discussion of the beauties and intriguing facets to the west of Cape Porpoise. Added will be historical notes and local attractions. If you follow closely now, you will at least be *tempted* to stop and have a look along here.

We can characterize the western twenty-five miles of the coast as being a beach, backed with wetlands. The beach is the finest on the Atlantic, ranking just slightly above the great Long Island beaches and the beaches of the Carolinas, and certainly above the beaches of Florida. The wetlands, the low and tolerably marshy country behind, is a wilderness wonderland. Wetlands are the nesting and breeding ground of so much wildlife that naturalists of this country have put forth a concerted effort to have them set aside and saved. The wetlands from Kittery to Portland have become a signal success for the naturalists' campaign. These lands have just been set aside and thus saved from burial under the land developer's fill. This will preserve not only obvious denizens of these wetlands such as the black duck, black-crowned night heron, rail, and other shore birds but the spawn of many species of game fish.

Now for the cruise data.

Crossing the border into Maine on a fair day when you have promise of more fair weather you should anchor in the Isles of Shoals, a group that lies at sea six miles southeast of Kittery. The Isles of Shoals have a big open fair-weather harbor known as Gosport; it is formed by the breakwaters that connect four of the islands, Malaga, Smuttynose (oh, perfect name!), Cedar, and Star Islands. This group is all by itself out at sea and is a sensational landfall.

Among the guides to these islands are a couple of volumes of information pertinent to the Maine coast. Yachtsmen call them the "Coast Pilot" and "The

Nubble Light, York
on the Western Coast

Bible." They are, respectively, *The Atlantic Coast Pilot No. 1,* put out by the U.S. Coast and Geodetic Survey of the Department of Commerce in Washington, D.C., and *Cruising Guide to the New England Coast,* also known as "Duncan and Blanchard" for its senior authors. *Cruising Guide* is put out by Dodd, Mead and Company of New York and the latest edition was in 1965.

From these two volumes, you can get navigation tips, shore characteristics, a rundown on the advantages of each port, and detail on supplies available. Neither book attempts to give a coherent cruise plan as we are doing here, but both are so valuable as reference volumes that no good cruising hull in these waters is complete without them.

From the *Coast Pilot,* you can learn that Captain John Smith stopped by the Isles of Shoals in 1614 and left his own name on the islands. (Fortunately, the more poetic and later name of Isles of Shoals stuck and we were spared "Smith's Isles.") You also learn that the state boundary passes through the middle of Gosport Harbor, so this is where you first cross into Maine. From the *Cruising Guide* you can learn that Lunging Island, one of the islands here, was the base of the London Company, a commercial fishing outfit that arrived right after Smith's exploration and very likely made a lot of money because there were fish for the asking all over these waters in the early days. In fact, the name, Isles of Shoals, refers to the fishes' habit of "schooling" or "shoaling" near the islands.

Natural advantages aside, island locations were favored by companies because occasionally the Indians would go bad-tempered and cause consternation on the mainland.

The Isles of Shoals was also, the *Cruising Guide* says, one of the favored treasure repositories of the pirate clan. One old sea captain accidentally found a hoard of silver here in 1800 and he was subsequently

able to have the first of Gosport Harbor's breakwaters built with the proceeds.

The Isles of Shoals have a bleak and, on that account, rather satisfyingly adventurous character to them. There are few people here and almost no services for boat men. There is a hotel on Star Island which hosts clerical conventions and which will serve meals to yachtsmen on occasion.

Around the time of the Revolution, things were considerably less godly in the Isles of Shoals: the islanders fell into moral decline. They stopped going to church; in fact they eventually made a bonfire out of their "meeting house." They dispensed with a number of institutions, among them education, baptism, marriage, and monogamy. In description it quite resembled the kind of life in the South Sea Islands which —at that distance—we find idyllic. However, obviously that sort of thing wasn't going to be allowed off the coast of Maine. Sooner or later emissaries of respectability came out and quieted things down.

The Isles of Shoals are only your first choice for a port on the Maine border, however.

If you cross into Maine on an evening with a hard surge coming in from the sea or with promise of a blow in the morning, one should unhesitatingly turn left, and so choose Portsmouth Harbor up at the mouth of the Piscataqua River. Head for Pepperell Cove in the village of Kittery Point. This is the first cove on the right, behind Gerrish Island. Here there are guest moorings, gas pumps (which we had used on our first morning), boat yards, floats, and supplies ashore. The bottom here is good soft anchoring ground. If the sea in the harbor is rolling, however, move up the river toward Kittery itself.

Kittery is easily one of the most historic towns on the coast. The Pepperell family, originally fishermen in the Isles of Shoals, moved ashore at Kittery Point and founded the first and biggest economic dynasty that ever existed in Maine. William Pepperell put together fishing, lumber, textiles, and shipbuilding and led an expeditionary force for the British, to become both a baronet and a tycoon. In Kittery township today stands the "Lady Pepperell House," built in 1682 for William's widow (her name survives as a textile trademark), plus the ruin of a house in which William was born, out on Kittery Point, plus the Sparhawk House in Kittery itself, built in 1742 for a Pepperell son-in-law. All in all, this is a great town for those who like to see old, distinguished houses.

Thanks partly to Pepperell, Kittery was a boat building town. By 1820 more boats had been built on the Piscataqua shore than in any other American town. In 1690, the *Falkland* was launched off Badger Island on the Piscataqua River at a point near Kittery; it was the first full ship built in the Colonies. In 1776, the *Raleigh* was built here, the first naval vessel produced in America. Paul Jones's famous *Ranger*, which took the first foreign salute ever given to a United States vessel, was launched in 1777 at Kittery.

Up the river from Kittery lies Portsmouth, New Hampshire. Up from that again, the river splits into branches; it becomes an interior tidal basin owning a shoreline more than one hundred miles long. This basin extends from Somerset, Maine, on the north to Durham, New Hampshire, on the west and Exeter, New Hampshire, on the south; it depends on which branch you take.

Because of its nature, this basin was the cradle of a rather exotic sailcraft design: the rare-looking and shoal-craft spoonbilled "gundalows." One gundalow could propel thirty-five tons of cargo under sail down to the coast for transshipment to oceangoing vessels. There is a model of a Piscataqua gundalow in the Smithsonian Institution in Washington, D.C.

Howard I. Chapelle, in his classic *American Small Sailing Craft*, describes the Piscataqua gundalow as follows: ". . . single leeboard, open or halfdecked scow . . . a very short mast to which is slung an almost vertical yard carrying a triangular loose-footed sail . . . the purpose of the rig, now extinct, was to allow the spar and sail to be easily dipped to pass under a low bridge at the entrance of Great Bay . . . and other bridges upriver."

Sarah Orne Jewett, one of Maine's more renowned authors, was born on the shore of the basin at South Berwick and she once wrote she had counted twenty-four gundalows at the landing there.

Miss Jewett's reputation has outlasted the gundalow's. The boat is extinct; Jewett's *Land of the Pointed Firs* and *The Country Doctor* are still considered classics of regional writing. (Both Chapelle and Jewett are published by W. W. Norton of New York, for those interested in pursuing the various aspects of Maine available in texts.)

Next east of Kittery is York, as you will see if you refer to Map Three on page 32. The York River affords a fair anchorage. Except for Cape Porpoise, it is the only real harbor of refuge between Kittery and Portland. York has the oldest extant public building in the country: a jail, or as it was known at that time (1653), a "gaol." In those less squeamish days, ten lashes were part of the entrance requirements, added gratis to your sentence. Today, York Gaol is a museum but the essentially dour atmosphere of the stone cells and sawblade bars still comes through.

On the coast, the York beach is marvelous and so are the towns scattered along the shore (besides York there are York Harbor, York Village, York Beach). They are examples of how to survive intact by use of intelligent zoning laws.

Once in history, York had a notoriously strident preacher, one Father Moody. His words about a fashionable matron who insisted upon high dress for church services are still quotable: "Here she comes, top and

*Old York Gaol,*
*the country's oldest*
*public building*

topgallant, rigged most beautifully and sailing most majestically," thundered Father Moody as she strode in. Then he added, not a whit more softly, "But she has a leak that will sink her to hell!"

Now we go up the coast again.

East of the Yorks, we first have Cape Neddick with a harbor that's not much to brag about, but it is a possible shelter from a southerly and on quiet days, a very restful spot. East of that again (going up the coast is always going east) we have Ogunquit and its small harbor, Perkins Cove. The cove is protected but you have to get under a drawbridge (fifteen-foot) and through a channel which is only three feet deep at low tide.

Perkins Cove is an artists' summer colony that has a great many artists' decorative summer houses along the shores. These are not in the main stream of Maine architectural tradition but have their charm all the same. You can charter deep-sea fishing boats here and the fishing is good. The beach at Ogunquit has spectacular dunes. The water is much warmer here than farther north, so Ogunquit is Class A swimming.

From a yachtsman's point of view, as I indicated in the previous chapter, the harbor is tough to get into on stormy days. As the *Coast Pilot* warns, no attempt to enter should be made if a sea is worked up, nor two days after a heavy blow, for heavy surf continues to break across the cove entrance in such a way as to cause a small boat to broach. To be more graphic, she may get turned sidewise to a surfing wave and get rolled over so she ends up deck-down on the beach.

Wells is the next town eastward: Wells Inlet has an eight-foot depth and a couple of jetties to protect the entrance. It is a nice harbor but, personally, although the *Coast Pilot* is silent on the point, I would avoid it in breaking seas. This is beach country all along here and the surf really rides up when the bottom gets shoal. "The Bible" doesn't even mention Wells Inlet,

from which I take it that neither Blanchard nor Duncan nor Ware (latest to join the firm) has been in here. But it *is* here.

Towering over Wells and Ogunquit is Mount Agamenticus, a cone which rises an arresting 691 feet from the coastal plain. It has a ski area on it and machines to make its own snow in the winter.

Last on our list of ports en route to Cape Porpoise is Kennebunkport. This is the hometown of Maine's most famous modern novelist, Kenneth Roberts; he wrote *Northwest Passage* and he wrote about Kennebunkport under her Colonial name, *Arundel.* Kennebunkport also boasts a slightly senior writer, Booth Tarkington; he used to moor here in a decommissioned lumber schooner to do his writing (most famous: *Penrod and Sam,* a juvenile which was, for us Easterners at least, as important as *Tom Sawyer*).

Six shipyards here at Kennebunk Landing built 650 craft from 1800 to 1880, including 176 full ships, 172 brigs, and 200 schooners! Yet the entrance depth is four feet or a bit better at low tide. The harbor inside, however, is bigger than either that at Wells or Ogunquit. Your best bet is to go in at low tide when you can see the mud flats in the river. The water gets rough in the entrance to the inlet when the ebb tide opposes a southerly or when there are breaking seas outside.

To sum up the first twenty-five miles of the coast: it has places to go that are fun. But once you start east in earnest, you should give yourself ample time to get all the way from New Hampshire to Cape Porpoise. Then, should it blow up, you can always get in safely at Cape Porpoise. If the weather is clement and you want to spend a day or so on the beaches or wandering around one of these inspired little towns looking for old houses, antiques, or just pretty girls (handsome men if you're the other gender), you can idle away your time pleasurably and still make it to Cape Porpoise.

*Maine's beach coast,*
*Marginal Way, Ogunquit*

*A dory-full of alewives*
*with more coming into the nets*

TUESDAY, AUGUST 9. During our stay at Cape Porpoise, Al and I learned that we had been preceded to Cape Porpoise—it was a matter of 360 years—by Samuel de Champlain. He liked its snugness, according to his notes on it. He also noted that the place was alive with redwing and bobolink and was amazed at the great flock of wild pigeon (now extinct). John Smith arrived a bit later, and with his penchant for bestowing names, called it Cape Porpoise for the first time.

History shows that the Cape Porpoise men were less than friendly with the inhabitants of Saco (pronounced Sock-o), just east of here. And, in their turn, Sacoites considered the Cape men a bunch of roughnecks. Back in Colonial days, one Saco man was haled into court for exclaiming, "Must we be ruled by the rogues that come out of the rocks of Cape Porpoise?"

Cape Porpoise—together with almost every town in Maine (only four escaped)—was attacked during the French and Indian Wars in 1690. It was destroyed completely enough to satisfy even a Saco man.

Louise Dickinson Rich, the most popular of our later Maine authors, tells in her fascinating *The Coast of Maine* (Thomas Y. Crowell Company, New York) about the events that followed the town's destruction. The few survivors were those who got themselves down to the coast and out onto Stage Island north of town. The colonists' musket balls were all that kept the Indians from finishing off their grisly job. Finally, the ammunition started getting low and the Indians started making closer forays. Nicholas Morey, who was the town cripple, volunteered to try to get help. This meant rowing down to Portsmouth in a leaky dory in the black of night through the blockade of canoes. It was thirty miles. And he made it. Help arrived in time and Cape Porpoise survived.

We were glad it had.

In the light of the morning after our arrival, Cape Porpoise was a warming sight. This is where the subtle and pervasive ambience of the Maine coast first manifests itself. Here are the granite shores and surging water, the lobster-fishing craft and, yes, the pungency of lobster bait. Here the first large fleets of lobster buoys point with the tide and here you see herring dories rafted, their swept-up bows and sterns rocking. Cape Porpoise is where the pilings under the piers begin to rise to the eminence of veritable columns, like pillars of some ancient and crude yet strongly built temple.

Here voices of lobster fishermen ring measured and calm; their resonances set the tone of the place, not the quick, boisterous, and unsure notes of summer tourists or vacation yachtsmen. The air is at once freer and more businesslike. The fishermen going about their work proclaim a strong reality, an integration of man and his environment. For those who, like most of us, work at six or seven removes from this kind of thing, it is reassuring to watch people making a living directly from the elements.

The State of Maine has always been at pains to preserve this leavening of simple life by regulating in its favor. Many a politician claims close links to the ways of the sea. Recently one Maine legislator pronounced on his fitness to debate on lobster laws by restating an old put-down to his opponent: "Frank, I've wrung more salt water out of my socks than you've sailed over in your life."

Cape Porpoise is an obvious second port in Maine, after stopping near the border, even for a power boat. Bypassing Cape Porpoise means an immoderate sixty miles of steady going to get to Portland, the next good harbor.

The best cruises are informed by moderation. I have stout support in this.

Gerald Warner Brace, a native and a fine writer, has set his novels in Maine; he also has an "atmosphere" book on Maine, *Between Wind and Water* (W. W. Norton, New York). Brace's philosophy is moderation on the grounds (I concur) that haste makes for incompetent behaviour. "The bad sailor," he writes, "is continually persecuted by nature and chance. His food and water go bad; his sails blow out; his vessel leaks; the winds are against him . . . he has much to tell and he may write a fine book. But it is true that bad luck clusters around incompetence." Anyone who has sailed, even once, knows how deep this last sentence strikes.

At Cape Porpoise that second morning, Al and I had breakfast shortly after the departure of the lobster boats. This is an occurrence that usually takes place in Maine between five thirty and six thirty. It serves as a reliable if needlessly high-decibel alarm clock. This is particularly true if you are parked—as we were —seaward from the fleet. The fishermen putter along until they are nearly outside the anchorage and then they open up. I prefer to anchor *inside* the lobster boats when I can.

It was seven thirty by the time we had our coffee down and were rocking gently in that precious few minutes of solemn rest that precedes activities and decisions. We decided not to provision here: the village of Cape Porpoise is a taxi ride away (you *can* call a taxi from the float). We planned to pick up perishables at Prout's Neck.

"Nothing yesterday gave me any reason to respect the ocean any less," said Al, reflecting. I said that we might, according to the look of the fog bank outside the harbor, have another respect-increasing day ahead.

Fog or not, we decided to follow our cruise plan and try for Prout's Neck. It has a good anchorage in moderate weather and is on a very pretty jut of land. We were also looking forward to a good dinner at the Black Point Inn.

The fog was a palpable one. It cut visibility to less than half a mile. We pointed up the coast and ran at break-in speed, about ten miles an hour. Occasionally —this is also standard break-in procedure—we pushed the throttle up to the yacht's maximum cruising speed for a minute or two. At that, *Puff TMD* (Puff, The Magic Dragon) broke out on a full plane and went ahead at some 13 or 14 mph, good speed considering the third of a ton of gear aboard, the newness of the engines, and the weight of the fuel.

There aren't many times when a speed in excess of twenty will make sense on a smaller craft in Maine waters, and we hadn't aimed for more speed in planning our power or our hull. As we trundled along, our main concentration was on our Constellation compass, purchased from Danforth in Portland. Robert Ogg, the manager, had commented that "a small boat needs a better compass than a big one." And this is so. Our Constellation was fit for a fifty-footer, but I thought the investment the smartest we could make. A good big compass is steadier than a good small compass, anytime.

We slanted gracefully down into the wide valleys between the gentle swells remaining from yesterday's blow and rode easily up the steep sides to the wide round summits. (Today no crests at all crowned the tops.) We took our little white hollow of visibility with us. We regularly gave a short blast on our own horn, a shiny twelve-inch lung-powered model that gave off a satisfyingly penetrating warning. We heard other horns and marked their progress to make sure none intersected our course or seemed to be coming up astern. After a while, the sounds were like those made by a modern symphonette; the percussive atonality of the two or three horns added to our own created an intriguing theme.

We were headed for Fletcher Neck. Biddeford Pool, a coast town, lies on this point of land. (It is not to be confused with Biddeford, an industrial town a few miles inland.)

Our course on the chart lay just outside Fletcher Neck. It happened that, in actuality, our course on the water did not. We came abruptly upon an interruption: from out of the fog, a line of shore appeared and it ran almost at right angles to our course. Curses.

Visitations out of the fog are not uncommon in Maine if you are a fog-runner, as I tend to be. (It isn't much fun to stay in port in a fog, either.) I often set out with Hope and Faith as passengers but my embarrassment at the inevitable "incidents" never seems to diminish. It engenders a downright rage in me to come across a shore where my chart indicates I am *supposed* to be running in open water. ("The Bible" indicates that there may be a strong current in this area, so I had some excuse.)

Well, we had come in on the near side of Fletcher Neck. We ran in slow toward the dim shore to see if we could identify more exactly our position. The fathometer showed plenty of water. Then a single, fairly tall rock came at the port bow. On that, we hurriedly reversed engines. The rock was part of a group called (on the chart) the "Libbyshears," and looked plenty hefty enough to shear off a Libby—whatever that was —or anything else that might encounter it.

Assuming tentatively that I was right that this *was* the Libbyshears (you can identify a rock wrongly, too, in a fog), all we had to do was to hold visual contact with Fletcher Neck and then come around to the ocean side of the neck ("the foreside" it is called along the coast), take a heading through the fog to graze Wood Island beyond Fletcher Neck and we would have a tolerably accurate departure point for Prout's Neck, a few miles off. Half of navigation is to have an accurate departure point.

As it worked out, we took *Puff* around to Nun 2 off Fletcher Neck without any trouble (it's nice to have the mark come up with the right number on it) and we motored ahead quite calmly at about five miles an hour, taking a direct bead on an invisible Prout's Neck.

Inboard of us, as we passed the neck, lay Biddeford Pool on the foreside. And behind lay Biddeford Pool's port, Wood Island Harbor, an easy harbor to make except when there is an easterly blowing into it. Then there are liable to be breakers. There are supplies to be had as well as water and gas, plus good anchoring. However, the harbor is exposed to the east. Alfred Loomis, who has written perhaps the most famous of the Maine coast cruising logs (*Ranging the Maine Coast*, now out of print), had this to say about it.

". . . I, for one, dislike an anchorage such as Wood Island Harbor that is sheltered only from winds from certain directions. To seek shelter from a northeasterly and then to have the wind back around eight points and kick up a small sea that rocks the boat at her anchorage, that limits the use of the dinghy, and that keeps one's eyes turning constantly toward rocks and breakers to leeward is not, in my opinion, to know the delights of cruising."

On the other hand, Richard Vines, one of the early explorers, loved the place. Vines was the trusted lieutenant of Lord Popham, an Englishman who was busily trying to establish a first colony in Maine back in the early 1600s. Sadly, Popham's initial colony at Popham Beach failed. The embittered Popham colonists had sworn after they had gotten off the beach that it was *impossible* to spend the winter in Maine. (Many later residents have thoroughly agreed.) Vines proved the Popham colonists wrong, though; he spent a year in a wigwam on the shore of Biddeford Pool in command of a fishing fleet, and the year was 1616. Vines called the place Winter Harbor and he was so enamored of the beauty of the "pool"—Wood Island Harbor—and the beauty of Old Orchard Beach running up the coast from the pool that he returned later on to spend the rest of his days in this region.

A bit farther up the coast, the Saco River opens onto

*Thick o' fog outside*

*Prout's Neck: Alan Baker*
*studies his charts before dinghying*
*up the river for groceries*

the sea. Today it leads to the cities of Biddeford and
Saco, each on their own side of the river. Vines moved
up the river in 1618. He had gotten a land grant from
Sir Ferdinando Gorges who at the time owned the
whole of what is now Maine and then some. Vines con-
vened a legislature or "court" on the site of his settlement in 1636. It was the white man's first lawgiving in
Maine. The first law passed prohibited selling liquor to
Indians.

The town of Old Orchard, just east of the Saco
River, has one of the best sand beaches on the coast.
There is not much else to recommend the town. Thousands and thousands of people have come to believe
Old Orchard *is* Maine; to my taste, it is so commercial-
ized that the whole beach should eventually be em-
balmed *in toto* as an outstanding piece of Pop Art.

It is lined with fun houses and soft, frenetic people.
On the other hand, if you are really young and get a
big thing from carnivals, well, here is one.

In working our way past Old Orchard (invisible in
the fog that day) and setting course for Prout's Neck,
I again ignored the possibility of the reported current.
It might not be working the same on this side of the
neck as on the other and the distance to Prout's was
relatively short. My conclusion from much experience
is that you lose more landfalls through the fog while
allowing for alleged "currents," "wind effects" and
what-have-you than you lose through ignoring them.

Once we'd left Wood Island, our world was again
swathed in claustrophobic gray and we strained our
eyes to pick up Stratton Island, which should lie just to
port of the course. It did. (Stratton is a well-known
bird sanctuary.) From then on, we had not a single
lurking doubt we'd be in Prout's by noon. As it happened, we came up out of the fog on the anchorage at
noon on the nose. It was welcome. When you get right
down to it, three to four hours of fog-running is plenty.

Prout's Neck (as we bore in on it from the foggy

wall outside) seemed to have three or four different kinds of activity going on. A cruising fleet lay moored there, in part made up of visiting yachts. There were hulls of at least two one-design sailing classes making up local racing fleets. Ashore, on the grass about the float, there was a yacht club around which young men and ladies were disporting themselves—gray weather or no—in the various inimitable poses of young men and young ladies in each other's company. This, together with clipped lawns, faint battlements of larger buildings, and rows of old and well-trained trees beyond, meant that there was plenty of social life at Prout's.

We got gas from the dockmaster and fresh water from the hose. Then we asked for and got a guest mooring for three dollars a day. (It was one of the few moorings that we had to pay for in the course of the cruise.) We soon swung in a rich company of motor and sail yachts, all moored snug outside the float, while the fog hemmed out the rest of the world.

While I busied myself with the boat, Al took the dinghy up the nearby mouth of the Scarboro River, using the "folding Evinrude," a 3 hp engine (we called it "Kinky") which we kept neatly stored, like a ventriloquist's dummy, in its little valise under the helmsman's seat. Al was to run for Pine Point, a mile or so upstream, where there were grocery supplies, something Prout's Neck itself does not have. With a large chart and plastic cans (Al was going to get more stove fuel) tucked in, Al himself—and a fairly big fellow he is—settled in the middle seat. The dinghy, with its look-through hull, still seemed quite at ease and whirled off on its maiden voyage with considerable presence.

Al returned from his inland excursion and reported that (1) Pine Point was definitely not scenic, and (2) that the grocery situation was not splendiferous. However, he was able to get cooking fuel and a few basic perishables for breakfast the next morning.

Here and there in Maine are fine eating establishments along the shore. Black Point Inn, one-eighth of a mile from the float in along the Neck, has been justly famous for almost as long a time as there has been pleasure-boating on the coast. Al and I in coat and tie wandered up to the inn along the lovely rambling woods on the Neck, a walk of about twenty minutes. The inn is a fine and expensive-looking building, somewhat reminiscent of the more restrained of the great houses at Newport. Black Point's big dining room is a wonderfully spacious enclosure, beamed over with wood of such thickness and richness that the ceiling looks as if it had come from an illustration out of an architectural magazine. We made the most of our very civilized surroundings and menu: a delicious contrast to the two days of primitive cuisine.

Prout's Neck has a large touch of Newport in it—as we hiked back along the road from the inn, a couple of youngsters came biking by, flying down the road in high spirits, chasing one another as youngsters will. Each was impeccable in blue blazer, tie, white shorts.

There is a second eating place, just a little more relaxed than Black Point Inn—this is The Lodges, a central dining lodge surrounded by guest lodges, about an eighth of a mile in the opposite direction, toward the foreside of the Neck. The Lodges (still coat-and-tie) is elegant in a low-key but eminently New England way.

Peaceful Prout's Neck has a Colonial history as wild as the wildest West in television land: Maine was a frontier state long after the more southerly colonies were fairly settled and complacent.

In the 1600s and 1700s the Indians would—every ten to twenty years or so—attempt a sweep of the whole Maine coast to clean out the white man. Egged on by some incident with the English, or incited by the French in the north who had nothing to lose, the Indians would work their way south, doing their level best to leave not one paleface in operating condition along the entire coast.

A marker out on the Neck shows the site of the blockhouse where nine tough Maine men (of course they thought of themselves as English then) held off some five hundred Indians for a number of days in 1703, forcing the Indians to halt their march south. The nine held out until the siege was relieved and the Indians had to give up their little marathon massacre for the time being. Maine's version of the Alamo thus ended on a happy note.

Prout's Neck also contains a bird sanctuary given by Charles Homer in memory of his brother Winslow Homer; the latter lived and painted on Prout's Neck long enough to become one of the great artists of his time, or of any other, for that matter.

Homer was an archetypal artist; it behooves us to consider him a bit. He moved here in 1883 from New York. He was forty-seven and had gotten the desire to put city life behind for good. In 1883, Prout's Neck was still a remote headland. Homer built himself a studio overlooking the sea and lived absolutely alone, doing his own cooking and housework. He reveled in his self-sufficiency, once reporting that "Night before last, it was 12 below zero," adding, "My nearest neighbor is half a mile away—I am four miles from telegraph and PO & under a snow bank most of the time."

He also built himself a little painting shed with a big picture window. It had skids so it could be moved around from spot to spot, depending on the view he wanted. The cabin gave him a chance to paint stormy seas without losing his brushes in the wind. Homer was given to endless patience when it came to waiting for the right light. He had been known to keep a work on hand for seven or eight years, bringing it out only when conditions repeated themselves so he could be sure his effect was authentic.

He was a very warm friend to those nearest him in his family and noted for his kindnesses to Prout's Neck folk who stood in need of some kind of assistance on occasion. But his regard for his privacy was fierce; he was rude to all people who addressed him spontaneously. It was a measure of his driving need to become, as he did become, a consummate artist of the sea and its folk: his paintings of working fishermen and sea-drenched sailors have not been surpassed.

Unlike his most famous contemporaries, Homer found his mature strength in executing American scenes as unfancied and deceptively simple as the Maine coast he loved. Henry James wrote of Homer's treatment of his subjects, ". . . he has resolutely treated them as if they were pictorial . . . every inch as good as Capri or Tangier, and, to reward his audacity, he has incontestably succeeded."

To the end (he died at his studio in Prout's Neck when he was seventy-four), Homer was everlastingly New England. One of his habits was to reply to letters asking for his autograph by sending a white square with his name rubber-stamped on it. On one occasion a would-be biographer got the following answer to a proposal for doing Homer's life. Homer wrote, ". . . as the most interesting part of my life is of no concern to the public, I must decline to give you any particulars in regard to it."

*Wednesday, August 10.* We left Prout's Neck early. The fog had not yet given much thought to the weather report of the night before which had predicted lifting fog. We were faced with a solid gray pall; the oncoming swells made *Puff* rise and fall into the face of the gray with the motion of a gull sweeping upwind. But there was a good omen. The fog was thinner overhead. This meant that there was a good chance the fog would "scale off," or clear, during the day.

A slight pause here for some fog advice.

Generally speaking, if you want to cruise in spite of a fog, you should go offshore in the early morning; take

*Gulls scrambling for breakfast
off the stern, Prout's Neck*

*Dinghying ashore, Prout's Neck*

a loop course well outside the reefs and islands and then hope like hell that it will clear. Keep a dead-reckoning log (your speed, direction, etc.). If the fog doesn't clear by two or three o'clock, use your dead reckoning to start homing in on one of the horn signals handily placed every twenty miles or so along the coast. Once you hear the horn, you work your way inshore carefully. You are able to be careful because you have given yourself plenty of time to do it. The object is to arrive in harbor before the light goes. (Night-running in a fog is a heart-stopping job.)

On our second fog day, we bustled ahead at five to six knots: Our hull could spin in its own length and accelerate out of trouble. This is a good feeling to have when you are likely to cross a good number of commercial vessels of oceangoing size, headed west or holding a great circle course across the Atlantic, as is true near Portland. These vessels have good foghorns and they sound them religiously, but no big liner or cargo ship can be expected to maneuver briskly.

In our case, we were presently relieved of our horn blowing and fog watching: bright overhead materialized and the fog began to move off in front of us, finally running away to reveal the islands of Casco Bay far, far ahead, an almost solid phalanx of rocks, ledges, and land. To port beam now rose the wraith of the oft-painted Portland Head Light, commissioned in its original by order of G. Washington, President of the United States, and built in 1791.

Before we describe Portland and Casco Bay we need to digress and talk a little more about cruise itineraries.

There are lots of places on the coast where you can enjoyably go far inshore, upriver and deep into estuaries, and Casco Bay is such a place. But, as explained in chapter 2, our basic cruise course is predicated on a two-week time span, to be made in short hops. Therefore our main course is laid in a pretty straight line without too much in-and-out. I call this the SLIDE

*Map 5: Casco Bay*

*Main slide course designed to show off the beauties of the bay.*

1. Fore River, Portland. The Commercial Street docks.

2. Centerboard Yacht Club. Moorings available. Fairly quiet.

3. Peaks Island Harbor. For those who don't want to take a yacht in to Portland. Quiet, and there's a ferry connection to Portland every few hours.

4. Chebeague Bar. One of the hundreds of anchorages in the Casco Bay area. Good protection from south and west.

5. Prince Point.

6. Falmouth Foreside. Handy Boat Service is the most complete in Maine; home moorings also of the Portland Yacht Club. All very busy and yachty.

7. Ponce de León Landing. Ferry slip and yacht float on Cliff Island. Worth tying here and going ashore for a walk.

8. Cliff Island. Northeast shore here offers good protection.

9. Jewell Island. Pretty anchorage on an uninhabited island.

10. Harraseeket River, South Freeport. A harbor of refuge, supplies, yacht club moorings.

11. Potts Harbor, Harpswell Neck.

12. West Harpswell Harbor, Harpswell Neck.

13. Mackerel Cove, Bailey Island.

14. Gun Point Cove—Harpswell Sound—New Meadows River. Shallow-draft side trip route.

15. Quahog Bay. Stop 2 on SLIDE course. Great protection. Lobsters boiled at nearby Pinkham Point.

16. Cundys Harbor via Ridley Cove and the New Meadows River.

17. The Basin, Cape Small. Landlocked cove connected by a tide run to the New Meadows River.

18. Winnegance Bay, Cape Small. Another protected anchorage off the New Meadows River.

19. Mill Basin and Back Cove. Good exploring country.

20. Sebasco, Harbor Island. Anchorage and moorings by an inn.

21. Small Point Harbor, Cape Small. An inner and outer anchorage here presents shelter near the eastern edge of Casco.

22. Popham Beach. First anchorage inside the mouth of the Kennebec.

23. Parker Flats. Second anchorage up the Kennebec; somewhat more protected than Popham Beach.

24. SLIDE course to the rest of Maine's middle Coast going inside Seguin Island.

25. SLIDE course going outside Seguin to the rest of the middle coast (when the tide and the current of the Kennebec oppose each other, the course inside Seguin is usually very rough).

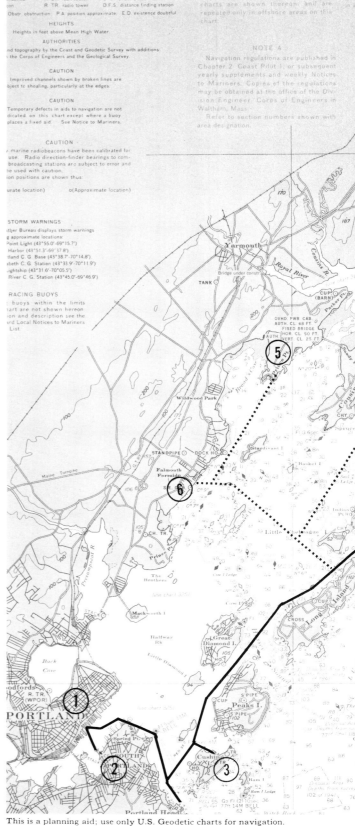

This is a planning aid; use only U.S. Geodetic charts for navigation.

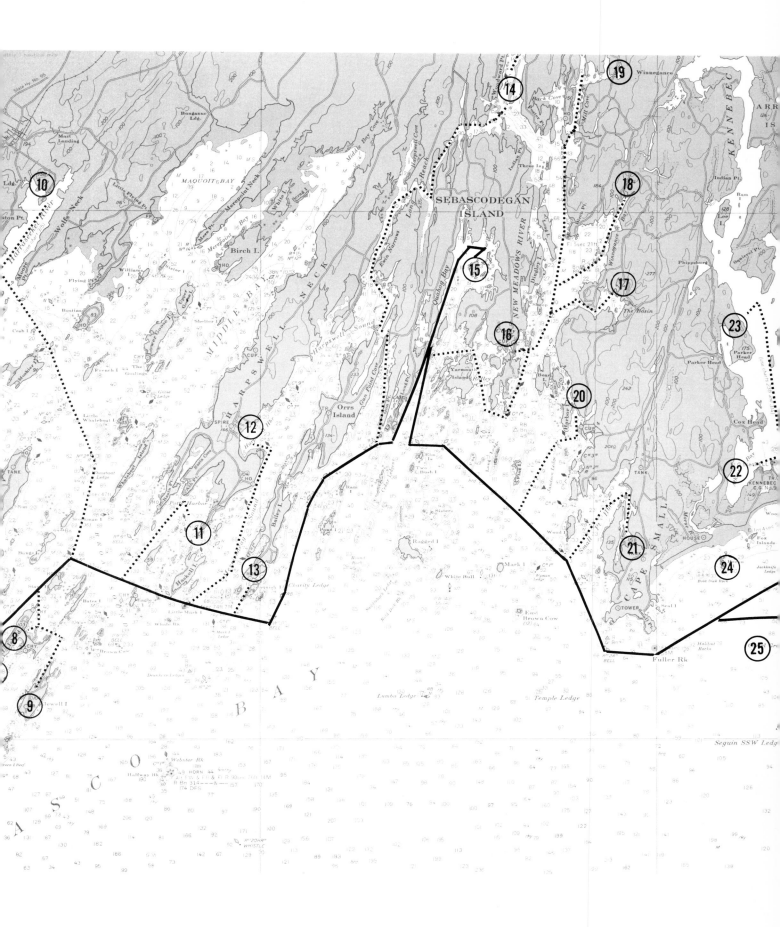

course (an acronym for the Straight-Line Interesting Down East course). The SLIDE course is planned to get you up the coast a maximum amount (and back out again) in two weeks and a weekend—16 days—having had A-1 Maine scenery all the way and covered two-thirds of the total distance to Canada. A better, sweeter sampling of the Maine coast you cannot get.

Additionally, there are side trips which will each add something to the cruise—each has a different experience to impart. The ideal is to cruise for two weeks on the main course if two weeks is all the time you have, and, if you have more, spend it on side trips.

With only a couple of weeks at your disposal, avoid especially the ten-miles-in-and-ten-miles-out run in favor of getting farther east more quickly. This way you will see more and have more time to enjoy what you see.

To address the specific question of Casco Bay: the SLIDE course (see Map Five, page 64) recommends you take a first stop at Peaks Island and then go to Pinkham Point, as lovely a place as there is in Casco. It suggests that other islands be taken as side trips only if your cruise is going to last more than two weeks.

Now back to our particular cruise.

As we approached the Casco Bay Islands outlying Portland, Al and I slid *Puff* into the big calm anchorage between Peaks and Cushing Islands. This bay is a likely takeoff place for Pinkham Point. Also, it is close to Portland. If you need to get supplies, you can take the ferry from the Peaks Island dock to Portland Harbor at the Customs House Wharf on Fore River.

Or, after you stop and rest, you can take your own yacht in to Fore River and tie up at the Chase-Leavitt pier. This was our option. Before leaving our anchorage, however, we had a welcome bowl of mushroom soup and some hardtack (actually Saltines), and then we cast off. We took *Puff* in to Chase-Leavitt, a pier just west of the State Ferry pier which in turn is just

west of the big stacks on the Portland (northern) side of Fore River. You can't miss the stacks.

At Chase-Leavitt there are usually floats that are empty for at least an hour or two. You can tie to a float and walk right out onto Commercial Street at the foot of the pier.

If you have any ship's goods to get, Commercial Street and environs are your best bet in the state of Maine.

The Harris Company on Commercial Street is a complete ship chandlery. Lines, anchors, shackles, thimbles . . . it is a heartwarming place for any skipper. Al and I shopped for a few smaller items there. I was irresistibly drawn to an alcohol-powered refrigerator which would have eliminated the ice problem. Of course it would have taken two days to get it fitted into the yacht, but . . .

Should you need a good outboard or inboard engineer, someone to install something complicated, or you have put a hole in your hull, the Albert G. Frost Company of South Portland, the firm which fitted *Puff* out beautifully, can be reached by phone and will have a man out to your yacht during the course of the day.

Gastronomically, there are two choices, each excellent in its own way, near Chase-Leavitt. One is Boone's Sandwich Shop on Exchange Street, a two-and-a-half-block walk from Chase-Leavitt. Here you have excellent breakfasts and lunches. Second is a better-known Boone's, the seafood specialty house which we visited, right on Custom House Wharf a few wharves down. After having collected some groceries via taxi, we got ice at the vending machine on Commercial Street and gassed up at the Harris Company dock next door to Chase-Leavitt.

The whole air of Commercial Street with its piers, chandleries, wharfside fish-unloading activities, and the commercial vessels loading and unloading is marvelously nautical. While gassing up at Harris, we had

watched two draggers come in and unload full holds of hake.

We then rewarded ourselves for a day's work by going in and having Boone's finnan haddie. In spite of a rough exterior, Boone's interior is lovingly finished and eminently respectable. Food: delicious.

After Boone's, we were ready to call it a day. Rather than go back out to Peaks, we motored over to the Centerboard Yacht Club, almost dead across the Fore River from Chase-Leavitt. In spite of reports to the contrary in Duncan and Blanchard and other places, we found the Centerboard Yacht Club's anchorage comfortable and quiet. There was a tug whistle or two but no lobster boats to disturb the peace. The club people are accommodating and moorings are usually no problem.

Another alternative would have been to go east some miles and lie off the Portland Yacht Club which is right next to Handy Boat Service at Falmouth Foreside. Falmouth is farther off the SLIDE course, however, and is noisier than Centerboard Yacht Club, believe it or not. There is constant activity ashore at the club and at Handy Boat Service. Besides, moorings are not plentiful. And float space is at a premium even during the week. This is the busiest pleasure-yacht haven on the coast.

Handy Boat Service has the following: good access to supplies, groceries, ice, water, fuel, and so on are immediately available. There is a small shower stall that can be rented, and you can take your meals at either the excellent restaurant at Handy Boat Service or at the Portland Yacht Club. Handy Boat Service has mechanics, a marine railway, and some ship's chandlery goods. (If you want to have work done, you should phone ahead to see if you can be scheduled.)

Portland, on the other hand, has transportation advantages: the city proper is a fine place to meet crews and to let crews off. Portland airport has jet service from Boston (one hour) and New York (two hours)

on Northeast Airlines. There is bus service to practically every eastern city and into New Hampshire and Vermont.

One of Portland's lesser known advantages is Monument Garage near Commercial Street at 190 Federal Street. You can leave your car here for a dollar a day. It's a very handy arrangement: for instance, I left my car here when I picked *Puff* up. Pat Bain, who was to come aboard farther east, simply flew in to Portland airport, took a limousine into Portland, picked up my car, and met us farther on. This same car was then driven back to Portland by the outgoing crew, Al. The car is thus available in Portland for the next contingent or for the end of the cruise if you end it at Portland. This sort of shuttle, using the Monument, has lots of applications to cruising schedules in Maine where there are very few airports along the coast. (There *is* a pretty good bus line which connects many of the ports on Route 1, but the bus does not get down to a number of ports, including Boothbay.)

So much for travel.

Al and I had decided to spend the evening ashore. We had both graduated from Bowdoin College, a famed and lusty campus east of Portland. There had been a lot of Portland boys in our classes and we called up one of them, a special friend, Hoddy Hildreth. (Among other things, Hoddy has become a senator in the Maine legislature since graduation.) Hoddy said, "Come on out." He is married to a fine girl and they inhabit a beautiful place on the shore in Falmouth Foreside. Hoddy entertained us with a number of Scotches and pleasantries on the state of the State of Maine and politics in general. Didn't we think Bobby Kennedy was a dangerous fellow? Well, from up here on Falmouth Foreside, which is like inside Republicansville looking out, we had to agree that young Bobby looked like a very dangerous fellow indeed.

"So," said Hoddy, "you're going up in an outboard cruiser?" That's right, we said. "Well," said Hoddy, "I

guess more and more are doing it. I get to harbors now where I never saw a boat before and now there are two or three of these little guys in there. Crowding the place up. Nothing personal." Indeed not. I agree with Hoddy. I, too, like to get someplace where there's no one else at anchor. Except that I don't much care whether I work my way in with sail or come bombing in by engine. Either way is fine by me. Hoddy holds out for sail, and that's all right, too.

Before we left, Hoddy had to show us his new charcoal cruising stove. He had it on display on his lawn. It was a beautiful gimbaled steel pot which would level off no matter how the ship pitched and rolled. It had a deep bowl formed so that the coals would heat up, piled high and close. "Steaks on that are just heaven," said Hoddy.

On that note we left for a rendezvous with a cousin of Hoddy's, Alice Rand, and her husband Pete, a promising research M.D. They live in Cape Elizabeth, just a few miles south of Portland.

Pete and Alice welcomed us with charcoal-grilled lamb chops and fixings. Pete, who is nothing if not a rabid Maine cruising man, took our thick roll of Maine charts, laid them down on his living room floor, and began what turned out to be a four-hour dissertation on the whys and wherefores of cruising the Maine coast.

We finished off the day by spending the night with another friend who had offered a nightcap and beds. Like many other executives in the area, Reul Taylor lives in one of the small communities outlying Portland and drives to work. There is still real farm country around Portland; Taylor's home, converted from a farmhouse by himself and his talented wife, Virginia, is half modern ranch, half Maine farm, and extremely charming. As a resident of deepest Manhattan, I could not help but feel a little twinge of envy of my Maine contemporaries who can have the best of city and country, so close to each other.

Portland, besides being a nice place to live near, is a place with a substantial claim on state and national history.

For one thing, it is the city of the early American poet, Henry Wadsworth Longfellow. HWL doesn't exactly swing with the modern beats such as Allen Ginsberg. But Longfellow—say what you will—made his lines *rhyme*. If you want a good head-nodding rhythm, why, open up *Hiawatha*. "On the shores of Gitchee Gummee, lived an Indian maiden . . ." if my memory serves. And *Evangeline*: "This is the forest primeval, the murmuring pines and the hemlocks, . . ." (We *had* to go over this one, stanza by stanza, in public school in Maine.) Not to mention the famous first lines, "Between the dark and the daylight, When night is beginning to lower, Comes a Pause in the day's occupations, that is known as the Children's Hour." Ah, well.

There are great sea stories to be told about Portland. Probably the best collection of them is in a now-out-of-print book, *The Maritime History of Maine*, by William Hutchinson Rowe, published by W. W. Norton in 1948. (A book-finding outfit—see your Sunday *New York Times Book Review* advertisements—can probably locate one for you and it will make good reading on any Maine cruise.)

Portland, early in the post-Revolutionary period, saw her crews "impressed" into English service on the subterfuge that some were really English citizens. During the War of 1812 against the British, Portland's privateers took revenge. Their fast vessels ravaged the British merchant fleet. The *Times* of London ran this piece (February, 1815): "The American cruisers daily enter in among our convoys, seize prizes in sight of those that should afford protection and if pursued 'put on their sea wings' and laugh at the clumsy British pursuers. To what is this owing? Cannot we build ships? . . . It must be encouraging to Mr. Madison to read the logs of his cruisers. If they fight they are sure

to conquer; if they fly, they are sure to escape."

They had really learned to build ships in Maine by then.

A couple of Portland merchants, Seward and Samuel Porter, built a fine privateer named *Dash;* she sent in fifteen prizes in seven cruises. *Dash* was hailed as a ship that ". . . never suffered defeat, never attacked an enemy's ship in vain, was never injured by hostile shot and knew no equal in speed." She also made her owners several hundreds of thousands of dollars richer.

In spite of all this, *Dash* ran afoul of nature. She disappeared one night off Portland near George's Bank while sailing on a speed trial against another privateer. She went down mysteriously without a trace and so did her sixty able men. She has become the Maine equivalent of the ghostly *Flying Dutchman*. A ghost *Dash* has been seen to put full-rigged into various harbors and then to fade away like a scaling fog. John Greenleaf Whittier, the New Hampshire poet, seized on this saga and made it into a popular poem, "The Dead Ship of Harpswell." Harpswell was the last port into which she "ghosted."

Portland was of old a great center of the West Indies trade. West Indian rum and sweet molasses were prized in farms and towns of New England and were traded clear back to the western mountains of Vermont. In return Portland sent the Indies things like lumber, shingles, and tobacco. The British, who controlled the Indies trade routes, slammed the door when the Colonies got their independence but Yankee skippers soon were back as large-scale smugglers. Trade went on as before. A decade after the Revolution, Horatio, later Lord Nelson, found that the legal prohibition against Yankee vessels in British West Indies ports was honored in the breach. He wrote, "When I arrived in Barbadoes, the Bay was so full of American vessels . . . had I been set down from the air I should most assuredly have been convinced that I was in an American instead of a British port."

Portland also traded with the French Indies and the Spanish Indies, even though the latter was forbidden. Lumber from the Maine woods cost $8 a thousand feet on board and sold in Havana for $60 a thousand: Portland still has fine houses commemorating this kind of profit. The West Indies merchants of the late 1700s and early 1800s built the Cobb-Ingrham, Wingate, and Storer houses, well worth going to look at if you are interested in Colonial architecture.

From the observatory on top of Munjoy Hill in Portland on April 29, 1844, a statistically inclined onlooker counted *two hundred* sail headed out across the seas. They made, said the observer, "a fine sight in the offing." The Indies trade was big.

But such a trade wasn't as simple as loading a ship and making out your profit statement. Piracy was a way of life for a certain raffish element in the Indies; the practice was encouraged by officials of Britain and Spain who hated to see the Yankees down there. The pirates were ruthless and organized. They sometimes ran cooperative flotillas to surround and finish off Yankee merchantmen. If the captured crews were lucky, they were merely flogged and set adrift in longboats. A nest of pirate craft operating out of Cape Cruz caught the Maine brig *Cobbosseeconte* in 1822 and set her crew adrift four miles out from Morro Castle, Havana. (I mention this particular ship because she bears the name of the lake up the Kennebec River that is the goal of one of the side trips in this book.) In the same year the entire crew of the Portland brig *Mechanic* was taken off by pirates and systematically put to death. But New Englanders were willing to pay well for their molasses and good men risked their necks for it. ". . . without molasses, no lumberman could be happy in the unsweetened wilderness," wrote one observer of Maine logging camps. "Pork lubricates his joints and molasses gives tenacity to his muscles."

*Tingling view in the Maine fog*

# CHAPTER IV

# Casco and the Kennebec

THURSDAY, AUGUST 11. Once bitten by fog, the first thing you do is look out for it. In the gray of the dawn, I rolled over in my bunk as *Puff* lay off the Centerboard Yacht Club and next took a quick-step reconnaissance outside. It wasn't bad and it wasn't good. The billow of fog had receded to a discreet distance outside Portland Harbor. I could make out a few islands of Casco Bay but there were more islands hidden than visible.

"Heavens, there's a little light up there," said Al, coming out on deck, pointing to a hole overhead.

That was at least something.

We had breakfast and the very act of breakfasting was joyous. I was beginning to reach that state where my muscles were responding as instantly to command as a nine-year-old's. Being on a cruise is like being in perpetual calisthenics—about the third or fourth day out the desk-induced tensions depart from the muscles and you hop about like a spring lamb. And there is the return of the all-American appetite. Not the hunger from unaccustomed exercise that you have the first day, but the honest savoring of the bouquet of the food. This morning ordinary sunny-side-ups carried the complete conviction of being the best eggs that I had ever tasted.

The incidental benefits of cruising (come to think of it, maybe the *main* benefits) were beginning to accrue.

Casco Bay is a marvelous mélange of islands. But even with our four-week allotment of time, we decided to pick carefully at this point among the plenteous dishes of the repast here set forth for island gourmets. The basic course, for the two-week cruise plan, calls for a run inside the outer islands to Pinkham Point and for overnighting in the fine protection of adjacent Quahog Bay. With an early start, we would have time to idle about in the storied islands off Portland, check in at Pinkham, and take a run around some of the inland arms near Pinkham, and still not use more than one

day.

Coming out of the Fore River, we coasted past Fort Gorges, squat and formidable with dour gunports, bush-and-grass-grown ramparts, all almost hiding little Hog Island on which it stands.

In Casco, almost every island has a story. And that starts with poor old Hog. Fort Gorges, named for "the father of Maine," the aforementioned Ferdinando who was given Maine as a proprietorship, was built in 1858 by order of the then Secretary of War, Jefferson Davis, later president of the Confederacy. The man and the fort had an equally unlucky life. Fort Gorges was never fired upon nor did it fire a shot, and right after the Civil War it was abandoned and is slowly falling down.

To starboard as we went out was House Island over which towers Fort Scammell, erected four years after Fort Gorges, also to protect Portland Harbor. It was likewise never used and is likewise abandoned. There is on House Island a small ruin of a stone hut built by the ever-present early European fishermen, dated 1661. Only one man, a solitary, has lived on the island, John Norwood, "the hermit of House Island," and he is long gone.

Close on the far side, blending into House Island as we go by is Cushing (to confuse things, *this* was once called "House Island"). On Cushing was built the first habitation in Casco, by Christopher Levett; he had been granted any six thousand acres he wanted in Maine by Gorges. In 1623, Levett spent the winter here on Cushing, another man fighting the vile canard that any colonist facing a Maine winter (a) starved to death, (b) froze to death, or (c) both. Now only an old cellar hole shows where the first Casco Bay house stood.

House, Cushing, Peaks, and Little Diamond, if you follow Map Five, protect the harbor off Peaks where we had anchored for lunch the day before. Levett is supposed to have used the harbor and called this four-

island region "Quack" which is as near a pronunciation of York (his native shire) as he could get the Indians to utter. He was a peaceable man and traded in friendly fashion with the Indians. As he was a man of compromise, "Quack" it was. The whole mainland area of what is now Maine's leading city very nearly became Quack. Luckily time intervened and a more dignified Portland came out the winner.

Just outside this four-island harbor of peaks, we turned *Puff* to a more northerly course. Peaks, incidentally, is the island on which the schooner *Helen Eliza* ran ashore in 1869, to be celebrated forever in (1) Longfellow's "The Wreck of the *Hesperus*" and (2) in little wise kids' remark, "You look like the wreck of the *Hesperus*." Or at least that's what they used to remark in the days when this was a favorite recital poem. (Do grade schools have "elocution" anymore?)

*Puff* passed Peaks to starboard and then Little Diamond and Great Diamond to port. The Diamonds have large trees, and kids, dogs, and people moving up and down grassy paths. It is ideal summer vacation territory. We motored past the eastern end of Great Diamond: it has a beautiful thick virgin forest that must look about the way it did in Levett's time. This is the Fort McKinley Reservation (now in private hands). We could see the faint outline of the fort's high edges as we coasted past. To starboard, at the end of Peaks, we saw a small islet with a house and wind-shaped trees that gave it the air of a small Greek island. (Carlton Mitchell, the only three-time winner of the Bermuda race, with his famous *Finisterre*, an incurably addicted cruising man, has compared the Maine coast with the Greek Islands.)

We now headed past Long Island, on our starboard beyond Peaks. Here a small green yawl with a long low classic hull and raised leeboards lay moored. We passed Ponce de León landing. Cars and trucks were down waiting for the Portland ferry to show. (We

could see her, the *Abenaki,* coming up astern with her low "dish" profile.) Along shore there were remains of the great fueling facilities for the Atlantic fleet in World War II, gone to rack and ruin, now used, *lèse majesté,* as a handy place to store lobster pots. The whole United States Fleet could handily berth in these waters. Off and on during World War II a good part of it did—those were the halcyon days. Now the Navy has left Long Island to its one hundred permanent inhabitants (many of them commute to Portland to work) and their summer visitors.

The Indians saw these islands as happy hunting grounds for the great clam. Clamshell heaps, some of them five thousand years old, are occasionally discovered when some soft mound is dug into. The Indian love of clam-eating was quickly caught by the settlers. Colonel Cushing settled on Long Island in 1735 to build a great mansion (ruins still extant) and invented a "clam boil" that he fed guests at his dinner parties; it was undoubtedly the precursor of all New England clam chowder. Maine's Long Islanders had a ditty which went, "Clam is my physic The year all through Come eat my clams. Bid the doctor adieu."

Now we swung on a brief dogleg seaward to pass between the Chebeague Islands and Long Island. Dead ahead lay Cliff Island, which was to be a stop for us. Historically Cliff is the locale of a certain Captain Keiff's grisly predilections. The story goes that he used to lure ships onto the reefs off the island with temporary lanterns hung as false signals for safe passage. Then he would loot the cargoes, kill off the survivors, and bury them in a field still known as Kieff's Garden: a veritable entrepreneur.

En route to Cliff, we passed the end of Hope Island. On Hope, there was the fantastic mansion built by the late Senator Elkins of Virginia. He evidently wanted to escape the Virginia summer, and what better place?

As we moved toward Cliff we could see the old-

*Peace, protection and*
*plenty of islands: Casco*

fashioned summer cottages at the waterside with high fronts and high second-floor porches. People were waiting at the landing for the *Abenaki* which was still astern of us. Al and I pulled up to the float near the pier (all these islands seem to keep a float handy for yachts at the landing wharves) to take a stroll through the inside of the island, which had been touted as pretty. It was. We walked up, past flowers swinging heavily over the dark green lawns, and were soon across the waist of the island to find ourselves looking over at Jewell Island and the sea which extended beyond that.

Below us, three long-legged piers, each with its stack of lobster pots, jutted into a small perfect harbor. A group of summer children, light as leaves, were dancing and diving off one pier, and as we stood there, others wrapped in their towels scrambled past us to get in on the fun.

There is no pungency like that of pines blown by sea wind.

As we took off for the float again, we fell in with a native, Johanna Von Teeling, a teacher in the Portland school system, who was living with her father on the island. She loves the island, winter or summer. As for the winter she told us, "I play lots of records. Music is my forte. With reading and correspondence with my friends, I hardly get time to do half the things I want."

I remarked on the two or three instances I had seen of old car bodies dumped on the shores of the islands. She said, "They use cars on these islands until they fall apart and then they abandon them. It costs fifteen dollars to ferry them ashore and what do you do with them then?" She recounted that she and some other residents had collected $100 to have the abandoned cars on Cliff Island picked up and sunk in the middle of the ocean but that one lobster fisherman pleaded hard for the cars, saying he needed them to make a breakwater for his beach. "So we gave them to him," she said, "and of course he just laid them out in a

couple feet of water so that now at half tide they are uncovered and look as bad as they did by the roadside."

We said goodbye at the wharf. The rim of the float was pretty well taken up with assorted kids standing about with a line in for mackerel. We coasted out of the nice warm lee of the shore brightened by a sun shining hazily behind clouds; we left behind the island, its families, and its peace. Here was a slow-moving summer paradise of the old sort, a way of summer life that had not changed much since the "verandas and villas" were built at the turn of the century.

The fog bank was starting to come back in and it got a bit cooler. We put on heavy sweaters before we rounded the black can off Stave Island Ledge and swung seaward again. Now we were in the open water on the rim of Casco Bay, heading for the end of Haskell Island and Bailey Island beyond, two points invisible in the myriad islands ahead: we'd round Bailey's to go into Pinkham and Quahog.

We moved *Puff's* twin Evinrudes up to full for the first sustained high speed running we'd done. *Puff* responded like a Thoroughbred to the touch of the whip. We went belting past Eagle Island, deeded to the explorer Peary: his proud white clapboard house is still standing.

Casco Bay was named either by the Indians who called this *Aucocisco,* (land of the heron), or by Esteban Gomez, the Spaniard, who called it *Casco* (helmet) back in the 1500s. The glaciers that once covered Maine moved south and west here, scouring out the long parallel ridges and valleys that became the intermingled land and sea of Casco.

At black-and-white Bell JI we headed in toward the mainland again (Map Five, page 64). Personally, I prefer to go from mark to mark rather than to rely on landmarks. For instance, here I went out a distance simply to make our turn at a mark. Particularly in the early part of the cruise, landmarks, such as island

*The* Hoi Ying *in home port:*
*South Freeport, Casco Bay*

bights, bays, and points, are amorphous and deceiving. If you make a practice of going from mark to mark, you will find that you clear up a lot of little confusions that arise. And this helps you develop confidence in that inordinately valuable sense of "third dimensionality" by which you project your chart onto the visible seascape by help of marks.

Now we were going up into our first real long inland arm on the coast; this was the Maine coast at its most beguiling. The ragged stretches of inland channels in this section, near Pinkham Point, are a match for scenery anywhere in Maine, much as other parts of the coast are praised.

By skipping some of the side trips possible (see the dotted lines on Map Five, page 64) before Pinkham, we were deliberately saving time for side trips farther north. My first Maine cruise, for instance, started in Harraseeket, the marvelous bay we were bypassing, inside Wolf Neck; here the Harraseeket River comes out at South Freeport.

That particular charter (will I ever forget?) was a little hull built in Hong Kong, the *Hoi Ying*. We picked her up from the owner; he showed us the sail list, checking off a "big" genny for the light airs, a "medium" one for the breezes, and a storm genny for the hard blows. We had arrived on the tail of the hurricane of 1959 and it *was* a hard blow. However, I had just come off a couple of ocean races so my ideas of what constituted big, medium, and storm sizes was a bit heroic. I remember that I picked out what seemed to me to be a storm genny, but couldn't find any others. So, we hoisted the "storm genny" and went sizzling out past the owner who was sitting on another yacht in the bay, watching. As I passed, I shouted, "Where'd you stow the big genny?" The owner blanched as we went by rail down because, as I found out later, we were flying it.

Pinkham Point and Pole Island form a gate to Quahog Bay: as we came up to the strait, we pulled in to-ward the docks of the Pinkham Point boat livery, one of the few places on the coast where day sailers and outboards are available for hire. There is a float and there are supplies, including lobster and clams, but excluding groceries. The company will cook the lobster and clams to order so we order two lobster and one peck to be cooked and ready by 6 P.M.

We then went over to the next float out which belongs to Guy Johnson's "Shrimp Lab" firm. (Guy was another of our Bowdoin contemporaries.) The shrimpers go out all winter to bring in the bodies. Guy Johnson's machines shell and pack them and he freezes them down and has them shipped all over the East. He usually has a few packages of delicious Shrimp Lab shrimp available in his freezer. We made a point of going ashore to see the plant, which was being overhauled in preparation for the next winter's work: Guy, a tall, balding elder statesman (although barely over forty) of the coast fishing world, brought the shrimp plant to Pinkham (a move now being copied on other parts of the coast), and he is looking further into the future. He feels that there is real income to be made supplying live biological specimens of marine life to schools and colleges around the country. He showed us a sampling of crabs, snails, and small fish that he was keeping in an aquarium, testing their ability to live under aquarium conditions. We spent a good fifteen to twenty minutes watching the hilarious antics of the scuttling crabs: they are lightning fast and react by attacking misanthropically and drastically any disturbing element in their ken. The wire-haired terriers of the sea.

It was now about one. We said goodbye and went off with a couple of Guy's "shrimp pies" (frozen shrimp in crust) which we melted for lunch. Enchanting taste.

Now our desire was to go inland, to explore the glorious, almost landlocked reaches for which the Quahog region—Orr's Island, and Harpswell Neck—is fam-

*Grabbing the pot buoy*

ous. (If you have a sail cruiser, you can rent an outboard from Pinkham Point for this marvelous inland tour.)

Following an itinerary suggested by Pete Rand, we set off from Pinkham about one-thirty, dressed in slickers and sou'westers to ward off the fog which sifted in from the sea and licked the surface of our foul weather gear.

We used lobster buoy navigation. You assume that the buoys are set in shoaling water (as most are) so that if you stay to the sea side of the pot markers you will be far enough off the bottom to get by. It is a system that works pretty well in the absence of other marks, especially in "thick o' fog." Most lobster buoys are set in at least ten to twelve feet of water, high tide depth, and many, of course, are set much deeper. In this latitude, that still gives you about six to four feet of water around the pots at low tide.

This day, the buoys bobbed brightly in the diffuse sun let through by the fog. I have often thought that the designs of Maine's cork, wood, glass, and balsa lobster pot buoys are worth recording: we passed orange oblongs with white whip-antennas on top; yellow boles with black and white floats on the whip; yellow cans with radiant kiss-me-in-the-dark orange feathers; blue and white milk bottle shapes; white feathers in chocolate jugs; blue and red striped top-shaped pots. If this were African art, it would sell for a bundle.

Now we were going into the deep recesses of the inner coast; we passed a green-hulled fishing boat, then a dragger, and then picked up a lobster fisherman who was hauling pots; now we spotted the ragged trees of Orr's Island to port. (You can follow our course on Map Five, page 64.) The fog had thinned a bit in here. We passed a couple of men fishing off the Gun Point shore; their lines were in the water and they were sitting in a pram tied to the stern of a herring dory.

Map 6: Sheepscot River to John's Bay

1. SLIDE course from the mouth of the Kennebec and Seguin Island.

2. Newagen. Harbor near the famous inn at Newagen on Southport Island.

3. Hendrick's Harbor. First anchorage up the Sheepscot.

4. Harmon Harbor, Georgetown Island.

5. Five Islands Harbor, Georgetown Island.

6. Ebenecook Harbor, Southport Island.

7. Linekin Bay. One of the bays of Boothbay.

8. Boothbay Harbor. The harbor and the town, center of the whole region, a famous tourist and vacation territory.

9. Townsend Gut. Start of the inside passage from Boothbay to the Sheepscot and Kennebec Rivers.

10. Upper Sheepscot River.

11. Wiscasset. Old schooner port full of captains' homes.

12. Marsh River. The entrance from the Sheepscot River.

13 Goose Rock Passage. Second part of the inside passage from Boothbay to the Kennebec—leads to the Sasanoa River, a tide run.

14. Robinhood Cove off the Sasanoa River.

15. Hockomock Bay on the Sasanoa.

16. Upper Sasanoa.

17. Bath, on the Kennebec. This is a large city with floats available for small craft on the river's edge.

18. Merrymeeting Bay. Confluence of the Kennebec and Androscoggin Rivers.

19. Swan Island, Kennebec River. A game preserve with a large herd of deer; from here route goes to Augusta, Maine's capital.

20. SLIDE course to the Damariscotta River and East Boothbay.

21. Thread of Life. Course from the Damariscotta River to John's Bay.

22. Christmas Cove. Moorings and anchorage for deeper-draft yachts; pleasant vacation resort.

23. East Boothbay. Boat building center of the Middle Coast. Floats available at the yards for overnighting of yachts.

24. Damariscotta River. Route to the town of Damariscotta.

25. South Bristol. On the shallow-draft route to John's Bay; the SLIDE course to Pemaquid and New Harbor (see Map seven, page 104).

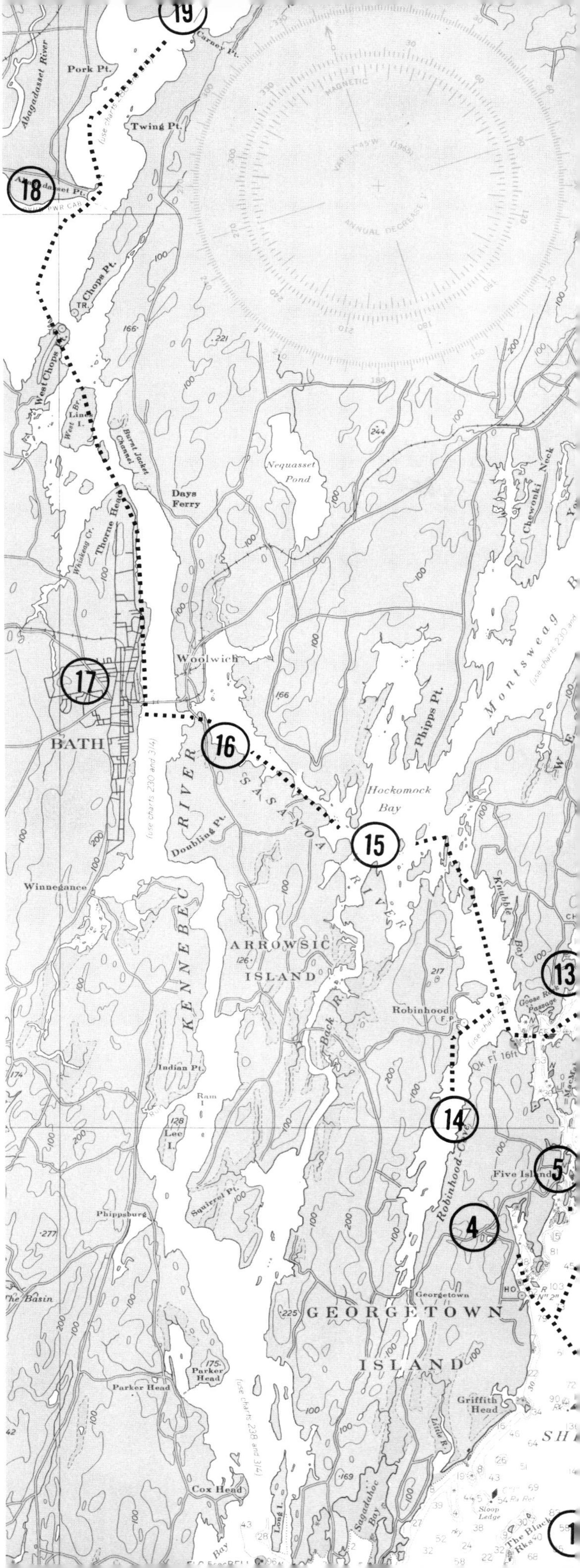

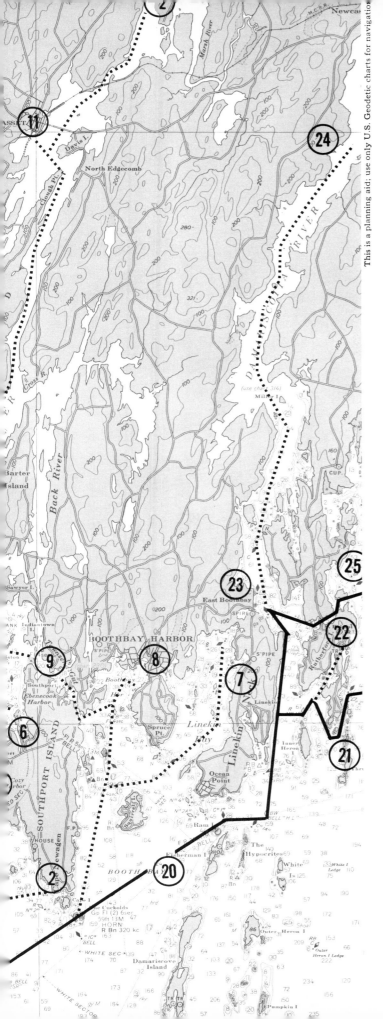

A couple of kids came zooming by in a small outboard and passed us, heading inshore, dodging among the reefs and ledges whose presence we did well to avoid completely.

At 1:55, we hit a seal herd. There were at least thirty harbor seal draped over the ridges of a ledge to port. The dull sunshine which had broken to the west limned the outline of broad backs. They watched us with a slow swing of their heads as we moved past. Then, when we slowed the boat and turned toward the island, they made preliminary crouching movements. As we got within fifty feet, they started hunching their way down to the water like so many fat puppies on weak legs; then they made their short flippered swan dive into the water's edge. It was a clean ledge in a very short time; all that remained of the herd was a few black dots: seal heads ducking up and down to keep us under surveillance.

By three o'clock, the sun was coming out. The overhead shaded into dark blue and soon we were riding in a perfect Maine summer day, even though the fog was holding on the outside of the arms. It is worth remembering that on a foggy day, you may be able to have a great time exploring inland reaches in Casco where the sun shines even when there's a fog at sea.

To our left a narrow cut opened up to reveal a short concrete bridge. We tunneled through after a lobster boat. A pretty girl tourist, having stepped from the sightseeing bus on one end of the bridge, snapped our picture as we went under. There was a thirty-foot-wide run under the bridge (the separation between Orr's Island and Gun Point) and fourteen feet overhead.

On the rocks and ledges to starboard we had several regiments of cormorants, the fishing bird common to the coast. They are clowns of the sea world, a bit clumsy in getting airborne, always posturing with self-conscious leg or neck stretching; we left them behind and went full bore for Ewin Narrows leaving Dogs

Head in our wake, passing Uncle Zeke Island (a great name!) to starboard, and then slowing down so we'd pass the small island at the end of the arm to port. (*N.B.* Please do same if you are trying to emulate us.) Here is Prince Gurnet, a narrows where the tide runs strongly. (I have a feeling that "gurnet" is an old local name for a tide run or tide falls.) Up to the last moment, it looks here as if you are running into a swamp dead on, but you make a hard right and there the neck opens into Long Reach, one of the fairest spots in Maine.

The tide boiled around the hull in an insistent sibilance as we swept into Long Reach; then we found ourselves in a calm "sea lake." The opening of Prince Gurnet vanished into the underbrush behind us. We were in the dancing late-afternoon light of any deep-woods lake in Maine. Across from us and south stood the only cottage on the lake, the Chatterlee cottage, with a clipper-bowed ketch, *Hussy,* moored outside.

There was no surge in here, no memento of the sea, no strong drag of sea wind. We had left the sea and gone into that Maine the inland vacationers know.

This is Long Reach: it narrows as you go in. Toward the inward end of it we were running between two close shores. On the right hand rose a small ridgeline. On the crest, a lone sun worshiper, sitting for all the world like a sea-struck Thoreau meditating near a log cabin, turned his head slowly to gaze at us, his interruption.

Again, at the end of Long Reach you seem to be running up on dry land only to see, as you swing sharply right, that here at Gurnet Strait you have another narrow hallway to another of the interior rooms in this stately mansion of inland seas. A real tide wash ran under the low bridge (ten feet now at midtide, seven at low) at Gurnet Strait but we scurried through the low arches and found ourselves in the sun, and within the graceful curves of the shorelines of New

Meadows River.

To our left were a couple of floats belonging to the lobster fishermen of Gurnet, a four-or-five-man village. Here, too, are the nearest grocery stores to Pinkham Point—had we needed supplies we would have gone ashore and gotten them at the local grocers, both of which have a fair stock.

Two old schooners, thirty- and forty-foot, swung on moorings in the river (New Meadows is actually a salt-water reach here, not a river), and as we turned seaward down New Meadows to complete a round trip back to Pinkham Point and our waiting lobster, we ran past a young couple swimming on Fosters Point. The girl, stroking off the grassy shore, was wearing a bikini as modern as the schooners behind us were traditional. She gave us a friendly Maine coast wave of the arm as she swam, the sunlight snapping brilliantly in the drops raised by her arched arm. This was our augury, for as we looked toward the sea, the fog had finally been banished. A stout black horizon line now connected the shores at the mouth of the river. Good weather was coming in.

*Friday, August 12.* The next stop on the main SLIDE

cruise course, as I had laid it out, was at East Boothbay. But, en route to East Boothbay, we would take a day to try the side trip up the Kennebec River.

The lower part of the Kennebec, reached via Boothbay Harbor and Goose Rock Passage and a few other nooks and crannies, is the most beautiful river run on the coast.

Additionally, Augusta (the capital of the state), at the head of navigation on the Kennebec, would offer Al a good chance to take off for New York with the least possible complication; his week was up. And Augusta afforded a nice rendezvous spot for the new crew which was to be Pat Bain plus a couple of long-standing friends, Kim and Lorna Massie. (Some of Kim's shots are included in the book: he is a professional photographer).

*Puff* caught up with a lobster fisherman. I had always wanted to try getting aboard one of these while it was hauling pots, and so we asked permission.

The lobster fisherman (*always* call them "fishermen") said, "Shu-ah." He gave me a hand and I jumped, Leica and all, into the hull. He was about to pull a trap. To do so, he simply took the line from the pot buoy around the winch wheel on the side of the engine and up came the trap. But no lobster. Inside were snails, weed, and crab. (The latter bite like fury and are the reason lobster fishermen wear gloves, if they do. The crabs here have no commercial value.)

And on to the next trap. This was attached to the first, and did not have its own buoy. (Usually there are five to six or even ten traps to such a string.)

In the third trap, we got two lobster. Both were too short. (Any lobster fisherman who gets caught with a "short" can lose his license.) So they went back. By the time we had all six traps on the string piled up on the boat's gunwale, we had three lobster for a lot of work. This is normal.

To put his traps back in, our man simply heaved the

anchor and then started up. The traps, one after another, flew off the wide gunwale as the line ripped them back into the sea. Last of all went the buoy.

"Thanks," I said.

"Any time," said our man. And we left him.

As we left the circle of protection in Quahog Bay—jubilation! The Casco coast was sparkling in a spanking southwester with unlimited visibility—not a wisp of sea haze. This was one of those days on the Maine coast.

It is a forty-mile trip up the Kennebec and we were twenty miles from our intended turnoff into it. But *Puff* had been peaking at seventeen miles an hour and could average fifteen, so we were not in for a marathon by any means.

Once outside Casco, we caught some excellent helming practice because there were goodly swells coming in from the southwest. We were now confident enough of the yacht's seaworthiness so that we took her over the swells as fast as our constitution would permit. *Puff* flew up the back of the swells, leaped over the crests, and went booming down the front, throwing spray as if she were trying to recirculate the whole ocean in a single day.

With the right kind of guidance, you can avoid the broaching tendency of a powerboat (throttling back as you come down) and make impressive time over such a sea. All you need is a well-found yacht and an itch to get on with it. We had both.

But we took time to stop and photograph several yachts under way. A family of five or six were having the time of their lives off Boothbay Harbor, sailing a fiber glass yawl in the frolicsome sea. I could imagine how the tales of the six-year-old aboard would grow in retrospect. What more salutary experience than coasting Maine with your family at that age, particularly when father is as superb a sailor as this one seemed to be?

We shunted past a dragger, *Mary Ann*, rolling her

sides up and down like an overweight Victorian dowager trying to climb stairs. The crew gave us a merry wave as we came up on them. We circled once, shooting pictures. Then we headed off for Boothbay Harbor with the dragger following: in spite of her rotund looks and high freeboard, she could average somewhere around ten miles and we had to really move out to keep ahead of her.

By noon we were having oyster stew and fresh bluefish in the famous Brown's at Boothbay, one of the gastronomical high spots on the coast. We had come into Pierce Marine next door to Brown's and had taken on fresh water, gas, and oil. We had used Pierce's dockside phone to get in touch with the Evinrude people in Boothbay (I wanted to have a routine checkup to ensure that we would have smooth going the rest of the way).

Boothbay Harbor has for twenty years been, and still is, the center of tourism on the coast. Tourist boats ply here and there, charter fishing craft set off hourly, it seems, and the pleasure yachts sail and motor in and out in an endless and brightly lit stream. After lunch we had a chance to talk to Pierce himself at his marina and I queried him on the subject of wood hulls versus fiber glass. Pierce said, "I can sell wood much more easily up here. The experience of people who buy boats here in Maine is that wood works better. I have two or three fiber glass hulls now that I can't move. And I've sold all the wood hulls I can get my hands on. In fact, I've sold so many Grady-Whites that they are sending me to the Bahamas on a paid vacation as a reward."

I said that we certainly had had nothing but good work from our Grady-White—we'd already come twenty miles in big seas in two hours and we were ready for more.

My experiences in powerboats have left me with at least one firm theory: I am convinced that the advan-

tages of a powerboat are nullified unless the hull can go in a heavy sea without shaking the crew up so badly that they don't want to keep going. I remember one $50,000 hull that I had a ride on: she was big and she was a floating luxury hotel but she ran over the sea with much the same motion as a box falling downstairs. One day while I was on her, the skipper simply turned her around and went back into port rather than face what I would call a medium stiff chop.

The total work needed by our engines consisted of having the spark plugs changed: and so, at two thirty, full of Brown's absolutely unbeatable seafood and homemade cherry pie, Al and I set off across Boothbay Harbor for Townsend Gut, Goose Rock Passage, and the side trip to Augusta.

Townsend opens up just around a red nun on the western shore of Boothbay Harbor—as we came into the gut, we were almost immediately transported to a new, quiet world: a couple of sailboats coming down on us, slowly, and an outboard streaming by at close quarters filled out a canal-like scene—something out of Holland—with small vacation cottages lining either bank. It is its own small world of homes, farms, cottages, and floats, and scenes of picture book charm. The vacationers who own homes on the channels here have the advantages of the calm of any inland water plus the advantages of access to the varieties of the seacoast.

Townsend Gut ends in a narrow neck off Cameron Point where a red nun and a bell on shore let you out into Ebenecook Harbor, which runs north-south, just as Boothbay Harbor does. (Our course is on Map Six, page 84.) Reassured by the lines of lobster buoys

*Lobster tumble into
the shipping crate*

*The object of all the fuss:
a fighting mad crustacean*

next to Cameron Point, we took *Puff* close by the steep rocky shore and headed for the northern point of Boston Island across Ebenecook. The tide was down a bit, and we could see the big ledge north of Boston coming out of water: going between these two was like just escaping rock fingers clasped about the hull but—just as the chart said—the water in between was good and deep.

Now we were out on the Sheepscot River, another huge north-south bay (the passage to the Kennebec is composed alternately of north-south bays and narrow east-west passages), and our course was for the invisible opening of Goose Rock Passage. In the westering sun, even the beacon marker at the entrance on the other side of the dancing spark-struck wavelets of the Sheepscot was lost in the superabundance of light. I laid my course buoy to buoy knowing when amateur navigators like myself try trickier kinds of navigation, in the end, after having tried innumerable shortcuts, we go back to the safe slow method of laying courses buoy to buoy. In this case, it helped because we flew blind for a while. It was a few minutes before we could spot the beacon at Goose Rock Passage. Once in Goose, we barreled right for the next beacon, by the elbow in Goose Rock, then we turned north into Nubble Bay, another north-south body of water with—this day—the cumulus in great white heaps above the indescribably rich blue of the bay. We sped past the little island, Thomas' Toe and thence into Lower Hell Gate, a tide run between Willis and Beal Islands—here the tide was making sharp trickling sounds that even the engine noise didn't kill—the current cut and swirled under the hull. Here we caught and passed a lovely powerboat designed on lovely lobster boat lines and next we passed Bareneck Island smartly dressed in pine and birch. And so into Hockomock Bay at 3:15.

It was, with this strong westerly, in all probability rougher than a cob out on the Atlantic, but inside it was a smooth spurt over water that alternated between blue fire and smooth blue silk sheen. A half circle of can markers led us west over the Hockomock to the entrance to the Sasanoa River (really just a tide passage, which is the last throat before the Kennebec). We had worked our way miles and miles "inland" and now things got narrower. The passage was occasionally punctuated with white water, but today we were not at the hardest part of the tide run, and so we saw little but a calm stream; two boys stood fishing it as if in a freshwater river; the Sasanoa was dotted with islets and swaying grasses along the banks; it looked like bayou country. Upper Hell Gate, the strait between the beacon on Lime Rock and the eastern shore, *is* narrow. Here the current was white-flecked with a suggestion of potential power of tide running through such a gut. We were coming through at what should have been just the beginning of the tide so that there was no real adverse current. I would guess, however, that *Puff* or any boat with similar capabilities would have no trouble getting through here, even at the height of the tide run, if she observed careful navigation. Going up the lower Sasanoa is like taking a large hull through a medium large trout stream with very deep water and only a few rocks to watch for.

Once out of Upper Hell Gate, we were in the wider part of the Sasanoa and saw ahead of us, over the tree line, the twin towers of the Bath bridge. The Sasanoa narrows again just before it lets you out into the Kennebec through the fixed bridge across from Bath. Here was the Kennebec, once the route of the lordliest salmon runs in New England. Just as a hundred and fifty years before, Maine clipper ships were breathed into life, later the destroyers and DE's came off in assembly-line profusion in World War II, continuing the centuries-old skill of Maine shipwrights at Bath.

BATH IRON WORKS it said in large block letters over the complex across the river. A ship of war or two lay

*Blasting by Cameron Point,*
*on the inside passage to Augusta*

*Backlighting on the Sheepscot River*

berthed as we came up. We ran under the unique pulley and cable lift on the Bath bridge's center span and made a hard left. We stopped at Bath Fuel Company, the local Evinrude dealer, for an item: a six-foot oar for the dinghy. Ours had bounced out when its tie loosened in the course of our run that day (we didn't know exactly where).

The lower Kennebec is more sparsely settled than it was even in early pioneer times: here and there Maine summer cottages ("camps" as they call them in Maine) sit solidly on an island or a bank, but mostly it is a rolling, wide, clean river with islands and bars; nothing but woods stand along the shores. Being familiar with the fairly well-settled reaches of the river farther upstream (I was brought up in Augusta), it is a revelation to see the wilderness at the southern end.

At a big, bald, delicate gray-pink rock islet with a big green farm beyond, we turned north around Lines Island and through the narrows between West Chops and East Chops (two points of land) into Merrymeeting Bay, the most famous of Maine duck shooting grounds. It is the confluence of the Kennebec and the Androscoggin rivers, the two giant rivers of central Maine.

Merrymeeting is broad as a small ocean. Today, it was overhung by a brilliant scarlet-edged cloud which framed the dark purple curtain of a shower falling inland. We foamed ahead, both engines flat-out. At Swan Island, a game preserve, there were a few duck blinds. In the sky were a series of Rubens-like halos of clouds and a deepening dark blue sky shot with rays.

To our left on Swan, suddenly, we became aware of several dozen shapes in the pre-dusk some several hundred yards off, below a farm building. It was part of Swan Island's deer herd. At least thirty deer—does, fawns, and bucks—were feeding nose down in the great meadow. As we slowly turned toward them, they lifted their heads in an ensemble motion and loped off. The whole field seemed in graceful leaping motion.

On again. We passed the north end of Swan and could see Swan's float: the gamekeeper lives in the farmhouse and visitors can land here and go walking around, even get close to the deer, provided they don't make threatening gestures.

It was almost dusk and we were spotting the channel markers with less and less ease. But the channel was getting deeper as the tide came in and we had little trouble recognizing the right of way with our Raytheon depth finder tracking the channel. At Richmond, the first town of size, some of the magic goes out of the Kennebec. Not only is Richmond a town per se, but this marks the end of the clean water. From here on up, although the cities are now starting to work on the construction of sewage plants, the water is polluted. It is not a dense pollution, but the air is no longer so exhilarating and you sense through all the five enumerated senses and through some unenumerated ones that from here on north, the wild is not welcome.

As the moon came out, though, the Kennebec gave us a smooth silver surface of transcendent splendor. We passed Gardiner and drove past its fleet of white, stilled powerboats. North of that even the small breeze stopped and the river was a blue steel mirror. We were picking up our buoys by flashing a light down the channel now, and we were slowed to a modest six knots for the last few miles. The reflectors on the channel markers blinked back to give us the direction and we came around the last bend of the river below the Augusta dam with the friendly dome light of the Maine state capitol overhead.

To the left, past the high automobile bridge over the river at the south end of town, is a float and gangplank leading right into town. To the right are the stockade fence and blockhouses of Fort Western where Benedict Arnold many years ago took his longboats up the river and attacked the French and Indians in Canada.

*Flying Terns on Cobbosseecontee:*
*author's brother Jon at the helm*
*and his brother's son Will crewing.*
*Boats race in the Cobbosseecontee Yacht Club,*
*oldest inland yacht club in the U.S.*

SATURDAY, AUGUST 13. Today, at Augusta, I laid plans to pick among the remaining high points of the Middle Coast, the section which extends from Casco to the Penobscot. I was also waiting for my new crew. Meanwhile I provisioned the boat (Al was taking off, his vacation over). Any visiting yachtsman can just as easily get to a phone off the float on Water Street and call a taxi to load up with groceries.

The situation in Augusta is similar to that in many growing cities: the grocery stores have moved off the main street to the outskirts of the business district. There they spread great asphalt aprons over what used to be prime ball fields when I was growing up. (Even in Maine you can see the free open space that used to be near at hand growing scarcer and hard to get at for youngsters.)

There are easily available supplies in Augusta. The nearest grocery is less than a mile from the float and there is a fine hardware store—Husseys—on the east side of town across the bridge. This store carries marine as well as other kinds of hardware.

After revamping the layout of the boat in preparation for having four aboard, I stayed at my parents' summer place on Lake Cobbosseecontee (Indian for "land of the sturgeon") about seven miles from Augusta. For anyone visiting the capital, a trip around Lake Cobbossee in a rented hull (from the Cobbossee Marina on the eastern shore of the lake) is well worth it. The lake is about ten miles long and has as many charming passages as any similar size strip of coast on the salt water. My early navigating was all done here, among the large and small islands of the lake.

The interpenetration of land and water: this is the distinguishing characteristic of Maine. It is particularly accented in the Middle Coast. Here at Cobbossee, the Cobbossee Stream runs south into the Kennebec. The Kennebec runs south to the coast. North of Cobbossee a series of lakes takes you farther inland. This route

was a very important commercial channel before the advent of good roads. Three lighthouse foundations still stand on the lake to show where lights for the Cobbosseecontee freight ferry stood early in the last century.

All of Maine's large cities began life as river ports (except Portland which was and is a seaport): Augusta, Bangor, Lewiston-Auburn. The cargo sailers came up from the sea and lumber came down from the forests and they met on the rivers in some of the liveliest boomtown scenes in American history. At one point, Bangor on the Penobscot was bigger than Boston and growing faster. There was also fishing, and lots of it, in the rivers.

But the trees were cut away and the booms subsided. Next paper and textile factories rose to pour their effluvium into the rivers. Today hardly a respectable game fish will go up the Kennebec, Androscoggin, or Penobscot rivers. Boating and swimming on these rivers is quite inhibited. I wish for Maine that the clean-up they have just begun on their rivers would be accelerated and rushed to completion. It is the only state in the Union where cruising yachtsmen coming up from the coast have access to the interior in such a thorough and potentially enjoyable way. I wish that the rivers would run sweet again and the now non-existent Kennebec Salmon (whose name graces the cuisine of the best restaurants in the East but whose presence actually does not) would start surging up to Augusta again and that the citizens of the state would be able to swim and fish and sail in their own tidewater rivers once more.

*Sunday, August 14.* Al has left, Pat arrived. The Massies had reported that they'd be late and we made arrangements to meet at East Boothbay in the morning.

By 10 A.M., *Puff* was on her way back to the coast.

It was a gorgeous day. We ran past Swan, where there was no herd of deer visible this time. Historically, Swan Island was visited by the earliest colonists in Maine, men from the Popham Colony at the mouth of the Kennebec, in 1607. And Captain John Smith visited it in 1614. There were farmers and fishermen (often a man was both) on this big island until well into this century. As related in *The Maine Islands* (J. B. Lippincott Company, Philadelphia), one of the early rural family units was the Noble family; during an Indian raid in the 1750s, the entire family—mother, father, and children—were taken off to Canada as captives. We can trace their story from then on, because it became a matter of interest to sundry historians. The most romantic of the Noble family stories concerns three-year-old Fanny who was ransomed by a wealthy French family and treated as their own; when she was old enough for schooling, they put her in a fashionable convent. There she was discovered by relatives from the Colonies and forcibly repatriated (by then she thought of herself as French). She married a New Hampshireman, and presumably was resigned to her fate as an American.

Another Swan Island family, the Dumaresqs, built there in 1758. (Their house is still standing, if you want to see it.) And another, the Barkers, settled there just before the Revolution. One of their sons, Jacob, went on to become a New Orleans merchant; he bought a steam engine which he sold to Robert Fulton for the first steamboat voyage in history. The house passed to the Harwards and the last Harward, farmer and fisherman, was George Harward, a selectman on the island and a member of the Maine legislature until 1931. Even as late in history as George Harward's lifetime, fishing was a mainstay of the island's economy: shad and alewives were caught in great seines set about the island as they ran north in the Kennebec.

Swan's happy days left a few records: when the first elections were held in Maine, there were eighty-four Swan Islanders; when the schoolhouse was built, they paid the teachers a top of $2.50 a week to begin with but, with inflation and all, by 1867 the head of the school was getting $21 a month. Then the ferry service to the island was cut off, farming paid less, fishing went bad, and the islanders gradually sold out to the state until there were no more.

Before we get *Puff* out of the Kennebec, we have to mention the Popham colony at the mouth of the river. The colonists were sent over by the same Ferdinando Gorges mentioned earlier in the book: if the colony had succeeded, it would have had the honors now bestowed on the Plymouth colony as the earliest New England settlement that took root. But the colonists weren't prepared for the winter: a lot of them died; their bones lie under the sands of Popham Beach where the ruins of Fort Baldwin now stand. The living got out in the spring with the first boat. Luckily, Gorges, as we have seen, followed up by sending over Richard Vines who was a smart and tough fellow: Vines proved that Maine's winter could be coped with.

*Puff* made its turn to duck out of the Kennebec at Woolwich, the town across from Bath. One of Woolwich's sons is famous in history: William Phipps. Born in 1650, he was the twenty-sixth child of a Woolwich farm couple. However unpromising a start this was, William taught himself to build ships, then to captain them, then to read. He went into the West Indies trade and while at it located what he thought to be the site of some Spanish wrecks off Santo Domingo, wrecks reputed to hold a bundle of Spanish treasure. He crossed to England and got his King to back an expedition to recover the suspected treasure. The stuff was there all right, and after a lot of politics, plus a mutiny and a king's warrant for his arrest, Phipps got back to England with two million dollars' worth of bullion. He returned to the colonies as a millionaire, a

*Mitchell's Mesmerized Lobsters*

knight, and High Sheriff of Massachusetts (which included Maine in those days). He sailed off to fight the French and then got back here in time to stop the witch hunts in Massachusetts. Luckily for the witches, Phipps's superior intelligence disposed him to believe very little in the efficacy of witchcraft, so he let the witches out of the jails, discontinued the trials, and told the clergy that, from now on, witches were out of season.

By three thirty *Puff* was being jerked about a bit by the whirlpools of Lower Hell Gate. This was a harder tide than we'd hit coming up. But Pat was hardly bothered. She had crewed with me on a previous summer's jaunt down the shores of Long Island when we'd had a good half-gale going for two days and had to manage a light cruising trimaran together. This was a cruise on which during the course of four days (1) the engine quit, (2) the yacht dismasted, (3) a new mast was stepped, and (4) subsequently, the rudder lines snapped and we had to steer with a jury tiller. I was planning on a considerably quieter cruise for the next few weeks.

On our way to East Boothbay, we made a short stop at Tumbler Island, a small and cozy rock with a single house on it that has a full view of Boothbay Harbor, inside and out. It is owned by Cal Mitchell, a friend and a dedicated appreciator of this part of the coast. Cal, now a lively retired executive, was at home with his son-in-law, daughter, and grandchildren.

One of the games on Tumbler is watching the cruising types go over the rocks between Tumbler and the mainland: this passage is right on one short route to the inner harbor at Boothbay. If you take the passage dead center, at half tide or less, you will, three times out of five, slide your keel across a rock. (Of course, if you look at your chart, you will see that the correct course is next to Tumbler, not down the middle.) As we sat having drinks on the porch—sure enough—here came a

baby blue yawl, motoring in, smack down the middle. "He's going to hit," said Cal flatly, squinting with practiced eye across to the shore. "I've got five to one says he hits." Just then the yawl rose about eight inches. Half a second later, it bobbed down again. The crew ran to the rail and peered fearfully into the water; the engines went full astern and the yawl made a cautious right angle turn out of the rock pile while we cheered them on. "Rocks one, Boats zero," said Cal.

No other hulls appeared to want to take up the challenge so, after another drink, we watched Cal make his dinner lobsters stand on their heads. He hypnotized them by scratching them down the back. They could then be made to do a handstand, head down, resting meekly on their whiskers, claws limp and tails curled.

We said goodnight and shoved off for East Boothbay, around the corner, to await the Massies.

*Monday, August 15.* We awoke to a brilliant sun at 6 A.M. It was the finest weather so far on the cruise. East Boothbay has two or three working shipyards. We were berthed at the float belonging to the venerable Goudy and Stevens Boat Yard, one of the most famous shipyards on the coast. Goudy and Stevens invites cruising yachtsmen to come by and tie up and this is one reason why I like East Boothbay. G&S is currently building a replica of the *America;* the original was the yacht that first put the English on notice that we had racing skippers on this side of the Atlantic.

The original *America* won a big-fleet race around the Isle of Wight by such a margin that when the Queen of England, who was watching, asked which boat was second, her messenger replied, "There is no second, Your Highness." The British, Canadians, and Australians have been trying to retrieve the prize (now called the *America's* Cup) ever since. In something like twenty tries over a century and a half, they have not been able to do so. The latest *America* will sail as

*Kim and Lorna, welcome shipmates*

an ornamental adjunct to the seemingly never-ending series of cup races.

Next door to us at Goudy and Stevens was the Hodgdon Brothers Yard. Here the schooner *Bowdoin,* Commander Donald MacMillan's famous Arctic exploration vessel, was built. Berthed there at the moment was the *Blue Dolphin,* a companion vessel to the *Bowdoin* on her expeditions. (The *Bowdoin* is now berthed at the marine museum at Mystic, Connecticut.) Another of Hodgdon Brothers' works was the fleet of Town Class boats built around the 1940s. The Hodgdon "Townie" bought by my father is still in commission, thanks to a bit of fiber-glassing. Recently my father (he was seventy-two then) sailed her in a handicap race against the current crop of fiber glass Flying Terns on Lake Cobbossee and won, beating, among the Tern sailors, both his son and grandson.

*Puff* was berthed next to a behemoth Chris Craft Constellation whose owner strolled by with a hearty wave before ascending to the upper decks: we went ashore to do some shopping at the grocery on top of the hill behind the yard. Next wharf over had a lobster pound with excellent lobster and clams cooked to order. I ordered a batch of clams steamed up for lunch: I assumed, and rightly, that the Massies would be here by lunchtime. When I got back to *Puff,* holding a potful of steaming clams, Kim and Lorna were loading their gear aboard.

We sat and watched the Goudy and Stevens people putting together a steel fishing craft to be used on the Newfoundland banks. Beyond that we could see the tourist cars coming over the hill by the grocery and down into the harbor. One nice thing about the Maine coast from a tourism point of view is that, except for the small islands, anyone with a car can practically duplicate our trip along the coast by auto and ferry. If the auto-tourist and his family want to get out on the water they can rent outboards at such places as Pinkham Point, take tourist boats from Portland (the *Abenaki,* and others) and from Boothbay to the islands; in general, they can see about 75 percent of what we could see from the cockpit of a cruising yacht.

Kim and Lorna were welcome additions. Cruising together with four or more is a very close relationship in any case; quite soon any conseqeuntial incompatabilities come to the top—about four minutes after anchors aweigh. My advice is to include tried and tested friends only, such as have been with you on previous cruises, ski trips, or long overnight drives—experiences in which you get a good chance to see how your friends adapt to the inevitable accommodations that have to be made in close quarters. Some very nice people are just not cut out for this kind of thing. As indicated, however, Kim and Lorna are. They have the necessary overriding enthusiasm for seeing the new and the exciting.

As you can see by Map Seven, page 104, we were to skip possible side trips to Christmas Cove and Pemaquid River in favor of the side trips to New Harbor and Friendship. The former are both lovely places. (Had I been under sail, I probably would have gone into Christmas Cove rather than East Boothbay because of the shorter in-out distance involved and because it is such a beauty of a cove.)

Our initial run with *Puff* carried us across to the low bridge at South Bristol: this is one of the most elegant little passages on the coast and brings you from what is essentially the mouth of the Damariscotta River, on which East Boothbay sits, into the next bay, John's Bay, where the much smaller river, the Pemaquid, empties. This trip between is one of the joys that a powerboat can embrace without needing to wait for the swing bridge to be opened.

Pemaquid River is a very snug little harbor behind Fort Henry, a replica of the old battlements once built there by the aforementioned Sir William Phipps.

Phipps's fort was the third of four actual redoubts constructed here. The fact that all four were burned and leveled over the course of 250 years testifies to the turbulence of the history of the Middle Coast.

Also at Pemaquid is a fine lobster pound plus a great sand beach. Here I spent all of one day on an earlier cruise in great satisfaction at the quality of sand and sun. There are some diggings behind the beach which may interest the archeology-minded; evidently an early settlement of English trading and fishing merchants started well before the Popham colony existed. There were as many as two hundred houses and paved streets, and not a document worth mentioning survives to tell the story! Recently a skeleton in a breastplate was recovered from a grave in the area and there was importune speculation that it might be a Viking in armor. However, the armor has now been dated half a century later than the days when Vikings were on the Maine coast here, if indeed they ever were. (The location of the original Viking settlement in America has been fairly rigorously established as being a good deal farther north, in Newfoundland.) No one has come across any implement so characteristic that it can be definitely stated the Vikings later landed in Maine. If you wish immortality in archeological annals, all you have to do is find a Viking helmet under a rock here.

Now we headed out toward the sea at the entrance

*South Bristol: a lobster car
acts as a sunken cage
to keep lobster alive and fresh*

*South Bristol: homes of
the men who harvest the sea*

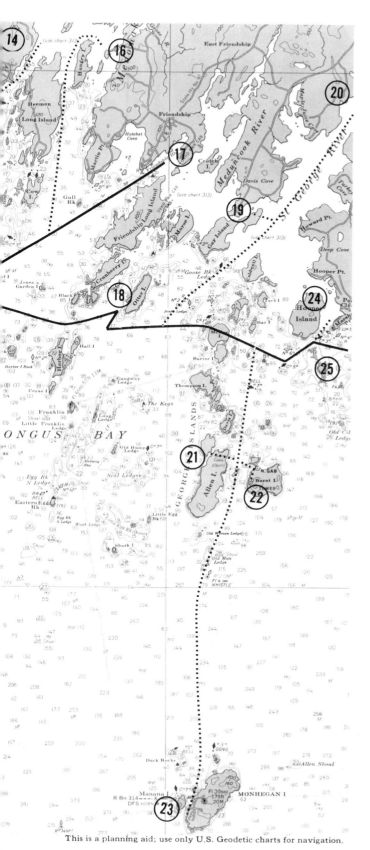

This is a planning aid; use only U.S. Geodetic charts for navigation.

*Map 7: Sheepscot Bay to Port Clyde*

1. SLIDE course from Seguin Island to the Kennebec.

2. Boothbay Harbor.

3. Inside Passage to the Kennebec from Boothbay.

4. Wiscasset on the Sheepscot River.

5. Christmas Cove.

6. Thread of Life. Passage to John's Bay from the Damariscotta River.

7. East Boothbay, on the Damariscotta River.

8. Damariscotta River to Damariscotta.

9. South Bristol on the inside passage to John's Bay.

10. Pemaquid River. Sheltered harbor off John's Bay near Pemaquid's sand beach

11. New Harbor. Lovely fishing village and harbor east of Pemaquid Point at the entrance to Muscongus Bay.

12. Round Pound. Harbor and anchorage up Muscongus Sound.

13. Upper Muscongus Sound inside Hockomock Point.

14. Bremen Long Island, on the passage from Muscongus Bay to the Medomak River; from here the river goes to Waldoboro.

15. Loud's Island. Anchorage and fishing village south of the Medomak River.

16. Black River Cove on the eastern channel to the Medomak River from Muscongus Bay.

17. Friendship Harbor and fishing village, home of the Friendship sloop.

18. Otter Island. Primitive anchorage in fair protection on an uninhabited island.

19. Pleasant Point Gut. Sheltered anchorage behind Gay Island in the passage between the Meduncook River and St. George River.

20. St. George River. The passage to Thomaston.

21. Georges Harbor. North of Allen's Island on the short route to Monhegan Island.

22. Burnt Island: anchorage off old Coast Guard Station en route to Monhegan.

23. Monhegan Island. Famous tourist goal and a fishing and summer-vacation town; an anchorage with only fair protection.

24. Port Clyde. Fishing village and harbor.

25. SLIDE course to Mosquito Island and Penobscot Bay (see Map Eight, page 112).

*The compleat clam digger:*
*having washed his basket*
*of gift clams he comes*
*ashore to turn them over*

to John's: by 3:45 the sun had started dimming behind a sea mist that rose skyward. We rounded the Pemaquid Point and went up into Muscongus Bay, which is the last of the subdivisions of the Middle Coast. (Map Eight, page 112.) We were at Loud's Island by four, intending to relax before going into New Harbor for dinner.

The harbor at Loud's is fairly shoal, bounded by Loud's Island itself, by the smaller Marsh Island and two islets, the larger of which is named Thief. It was so peaceful here that we threw in the anchor and just sat around. Loud's was once the home of the great sachem (Indian chief-of-state) Samoset and later was the site of Loudsville, an early fishing village. Loudsville is still there and is still pretty much the same as it was—over the knoll from the harbor—an old, proud settlement. On the small island next to Thief we could see a man busily digging clams.

Kim and I rowed the dinghy over to shoot pictures of him at work. He had a short-handled clam rake and was digging away with a speed that would have made one say he was frantic except that it was simply an example of practiced clam digging. Now and then he'd go stomping across the tide flats to see if he could spot the clams by the small jets of water which the pressure of the stomping caused the clams to jet out of their long feeding holes. These are tiny narrow tunnels leading down to the clam itself, buried in the sand; it simply lies there ingesting nutrient and expelling waste through the tunnel without having to move. Doubtless this accounts for the expression "happy as a clam."

Once he had located some jets, our man bent over quickly and attacked with atavistic fervor; he was a man intent on wresting food raw from the earth. Something there of Millet's *Man with a Hoe*. And something there of thousands of Abenaki and related tribes and, before them, the Red Paint men, clawing away the sand so they could eat, and leaving behind piles of clam

and mussel shells which in time became round mounds along the shore and in time were put through a carbon-dating process to show that man was foraging here in 2000 B.C.

We asked him what he was doing: he was, he said, "just getting a mess of clams." He was off the herring boat moored up near the shore and he was getting the crew some clams for a stew. We offered to buy some, but he refused. He said, "Here, I'll dig you a mess." And he attacked a new patch of mud flat, churned it up with the rake, and reached quick, hard hands down into the jumble of sand and mud, coming up with a clam every few seconds or so. They just seemed to jump into the space between his thumb and forefinger as in a conjurer's trick. He piled twenty or so up for us before we could persuade him to stop.

We rowed the dinghy back to the yacht with twenty of the biggest, meanest-looking clams I've seen. The wild clam's huge eating-and-expulsion extension, swollen with water, thrusts upward like a dwarf elephant's trunk, weed and sand clings to the shell, and the smell of the bottom is about him.

With the clams astern in a bucket, we set off, full power, for New Harbor where we had a rendezvous with some members of my family, including several cousins and nephews.

New Harbor is a perfect cleft in the side of Muscongus. It has a large active fishing fleet, two big floats under the town landing, fishermen's houses on all the banks and a quiet inner anchorage. Above the floats, a lobster pound serves steamed lobster and clams by the shovelful. We motored in to the float, tied up, and ascended to the restaurant.

There had to be a show ride for the youngsters: six of them piled in and I took them out around the bell off New Harbor and opened *Puff* up. "Is this as fast as she goes?" said Michael (a nephew), trying to hold back his chagrin. There is no impressing the space age youngster with anything less than Mach 1.

With night coming in, we double-anchored *Puff* in New Harbor's inner sanctuary which has been newly dredged to give New Harbor some much needed space for her visitors. We swung between two lobster boats. The solid sweeping lines of the working design contrasted nicely with the compound curves of our high-riding, light-sitting yacht.

*Tuesday, August 16.* I was awakened by a solid thump and looked out the ripply plastic window of the cockpit curtain to see a seagull staring at us from a muddy bank about eight feet away. The tides really run here at New Harbor. I kicked on the cabin door and told Kim to look out and watch us go dry. We speculated briefly on whether or not we'd shorten anchor and if that was or was not the props hitting. Tide was coming in (otherwise the entire basin and all its boats would obviously soon be dry). So we left it and swung on the end of what apparently was too much scope. It should be explained that scope is the ratio of length of anchor line to depth and that good scope is about five times depth, with more if you expect trouble. Kim had been in charge of scope the night before and I suggested that, with the scope he had allowed, we would soon be making a full turn of the harbor and sweeping the harbor clear of pots, boats, and moorings.

A morning fog laced itself around the harbor but it looked thin, a poltergeist of a fog, and would not last out the direct attack of the sun.

After breakfast we went back in to the float, gassed, chatted with a local lobster fisherman and learned that lobstering was bad all over; that the average lobsterman kept about three hundred traps out on the bottom, although it might go as high as five hundred; that he checked half of his pots each day and expected to average a pound of lobster a pot in good years; this year he was getting a pound for every three pots; that the

Russian trawlers off the coast were blamed by some for the decline of lobster boatings—they killed off the big seed lobster; that others believed the bigger deep-water lobster had nothing to do with the smaller inshore species. [We also were told that if you didn't peg a lobster's big claw, he could handily top your finger for you.]

We decided to take one more side trip, this one up to Friendship. The harbor is the home of the famous Friendship sloops, the predecessor of the motor lobster boat. The Friendship, with its bowsprit, big main sail, and often with double headsails, could be made to hang in the wind while her master tended pots, hauled a net, or did other fishing tasks at sea; she was as sturdy and sea-kindly as any hull ever built in Maine and that says a lot.

By 3:50 we were past the Ross and Haddock Islands, and by five into Friendship.

We went ashore at a commercial float belonging to Albert Roberts, standing now, at almost dead low tide, some twenty-five feet above the water on spindles of rough-hewn timber; a forty-foot gangplank came down to the float at an alarming angle. On the float, small fry and old fry were fishing for mackerel. When the mackerel are running in Friendship there is no age bar. One of the less tender ladies was sporting a battered fishing hat, smoking an angled cigarette, and making fifty-foot casts with a flick of her wrist that arched the line out in a perfect bow to windward.

Mrs. Roberts, at the top of the gangway, proved to be the secretary of the National Friendship Sloop Association. There is only one Friendship sloop now owned here. But every year there is the annual Friendship sloop race at Friendship when the Massachusetts owners and the Maine owners, as many as thirty owners in all, come here to see who is the best Friendship sloop sailor of them all. These are twenty-five- to thirty-five-footers (mostly around thirty), and they carry lots and

*Two auxiliaries preparing to anchor off*

*New Harbor: the guest*
*mooring in the inner harbor*

lots of canvas. Every time a Friendship comes into the harbor, Mrs. Roberts welcomes it with a blast from a small cannon set up on the outside stairs of the store.

Having gotten our gas, we asked if we could get to a hardware store—there were a few things that I needed. There was a store in town a few miles away and Mrs. Roberts said we could help ourselves to the pickup truck. This was a typical coast gesture of neighborliness: we took the truck and wound up the hill over the harbor and into the town. Here was an old-fashioned wood-smelling hardware store, but it had what I needed. We drove the pickup back and then took off for Otter Island, our chosen harbor for the night.

We were in for a bit of slow navigating as we headed for Otter in the fog. We felt our way around dimly seen shores until we found the south-running shore on the eastern side of Otter Island. We got down to the tip of it where the harbor notched into the coastline, offering us a welcome rest from fog navigation.

*Wednesday, August 17.* At 8 A.M. I woke to check our distance from the shore. We had double-anchored: this is not much more than a cove and it is less than one hundred feet wide. But the double-anchoring was holding us well clear of both walls. There was fog outside but as I sleepily switched on the Bendix radio direction finder and AM radio we got what seemed like a promising forecast: west winds and a lifting fog.

9 A.M.: Kim announced that Lorna refused to get up. I said that it was, after all, her vacation. I busied myself putting some angle irons on the dinghy seat brace while Pat cleared the deck for breakfast.

10 A.M.: Breakfast and general calm. The woods here ring with no ax nor sound with the gutteral staccato of the chain saw. Silvery light through the fog played on the rippling surface of the harbor, drawn into wrinkles by the slight westerly breeze.

10:30 A.M.: We decided to call a general swim. Kim

went first and came up to pronounce his general verdict of chilly but not icy. "Let me aboard," he added. But here the sun broke through and Kim soon felt warm enough for another dive. I went in and found it quite brisk. Lorna went in slowly, backward, down the boarding ladder, and then Pat. We are all heroes.

1 P.M.: The fog receded a bit. The next main SLIDE course stop was around the corner to Penobscot Bay and over to the Basin, a fascinating spot in the middle of the Penobscot. But since Kim and Lorna had to leave the cruise today, we were to take the side trip up the west shore of the bay that takes in Rockland, Camden, and Pulpit Harbor. (See Map Nine, page 116.) At either Rockland or Camden, the Massies would get a bus down U.S. Route 1 to the big cities on the coast.

We were off then, going into the fog and hoping that the weather prediction would work out. At 1:08 P.M. with the visibility lousy (about twenty-five feet to thirty-five feet maximum), we nevertheless hit dead-on our first mark, a lovely little red nun, solidifying out of the wet veil of gray at the end of a mile's run. Everyone gains confidence in their navigator, me.

From here we threaded between McGee and Seaves, between Hooper and Hart, past Marshall Ledge, and were almost around the corner into the Penobscot when we went off course. We fetched an island that was not on our calculated course at all.

There is nothing as fascinating as a little surprise islet out of the fog. You skitter about it, measure the height, eye the breadth, deliberate on its topography, and then admit you are off course; in order to get back, you have to identify this ugly piece of land. Our decision (and all decisions are somewhat arbitrary in fog) was that this was the bigger of the Two Brothers. We circled in behind and lo, the other Brother appeared and confirmed our diagnosis. How I got this far down from my course, I am not sure: there must be a strong local current that Duncan and Blanchard does not mention.

We went north of Mosquito Island to save a little time. This is a narrower channel than we would have found if we'd gone out around, but a narrow channel, if not too shoal, is easier to follow than a wider one: you know when you are off. And with the fog threatening to close in entirely on the bow, it looked like a long day to Camden. Any time saved would be welcome.

We hadn't gone far when we came on an arresting sight: a ledge awash in the fog. The swell off the ocean arose extra inches as if to hide the dark stained teeth of rock and then the swell broke and parted like a stage curtain, revealing in a rabid swirl of white the black ragged line of it jutting up, as if started from the depths.

In sum, I'd gone off course again, a bit to the north this time. I had been tempted to blame my error in the first instance on the compass or current and had started compensating, wanting to prove that I was right. All I proved was that (1) my compass was not deviating, and (2) there was no appreciable current. Again, the wisdom of ignoring "currents" became apparent.

While on the subject, there is another interesting deviation besides this "righteous deviation." The other kind I call "terra firma" deviation. This is when the helmsman tends to favor the side on which he last saw land. It is almost a tropism until the helmsman becomes fog-hardened.

Now we—oh joy!—gained Penobscot Bay proper: a left turn around Mosquito Head and we were off, slowly moving for Whitehead Island: the foghorn on the island would make this a fairly simple target; beyond that lay Muscle Ridge, one of the more tangled passages on the coast. As we ran on a course of 70, the visibility improved slightly so I opened up to about twelve miles an hour and we surged ahead. It was evident we would have a close thing to get to Camden by 5 P.M., the hour of departure of the bus. So we decided

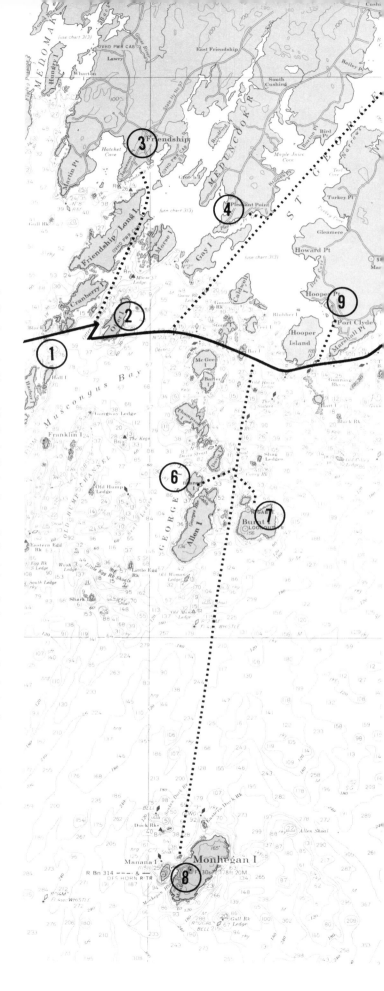

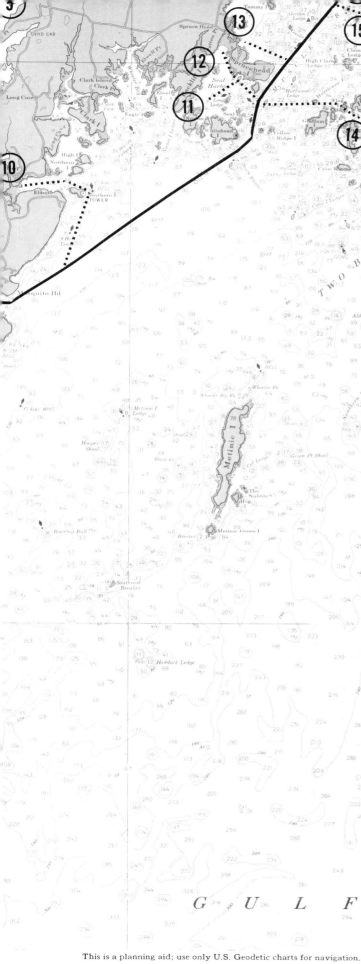

*Map 8: Friendship to Muscle Ridge*

1. SLIDE course from New Harbor and Loud's Island.

2. Otter Island. Cove on an uninhabited island.

3. Friendship. Town and anchorage.

4. Pleasant Point Gut. Protected passage and anchorage.

5. St. George River. Passage to Thomaston.

6. Georges Harbor on the route to Monhegan.

7. Burnt Island harbor on the route to Monhegan.

8. Monhegan Island. Tourist and vacation center.

9. Port Clyde, on the passage from Muscongus Bay to Penobscot Bay.

10. Tenant's Harbor. Well-protected harbor, first anchorage in the Penobscot.

11. Long Ledge anchorage, Seal Harbor. Protected from south and west.

12. Inner Seal Harbor. Protected from north and west.

13. Spruce Head anchorage. Protected from south and west.

14. Home Harbor in Muscle Ridge.

15. Dix Harbor in Muscle Ridge.

16. SLIDE course to Vinalhaven, Rockland, and Camden.

This is a planning aid; use only U.S. Geodetic charts for navigation.

to head the bus off at Rockland, not one of my favorite ports. However, we *were* on the Penobscot, one of the very special places on earth.

My exits and entrances to the Penobscot in the past seem to have been dogged with a certain fate. I remembered this in fog as we bypassed the fine little anchorage in Tenant's Harbor. A few years ago, a crew of us were in there, preparing to make our way out of the Penobscot in the morning. I had a small pressure gas stove which I only lit while it was on deck. In order to cook steaks that particular night, I decided we would get more heat out of the stove if I put it inside a tin bucket. The result was some sort of escalating cyclical reaction. The hitherto mouselike stove suddenly began to roar, lionlike. A real geyser of flame stood high over the rim of the bucket. One crew member hurriedly got out the boathook and dunked the whole thing over the side. But not soon enough. There was a small rim of charred wood on the beautiful mahogany seat. The rest of the trip, one crew member on each watch worked the Operation Erase detail, slowly but cunningly sanding out the circular mark. We returned the boat to the charterer minus the mark but with a slight concavity in his mahogany seat.

The next harbor north of note, which we were also bypassing, was Seal Harbor. The first time I ever made the Penobscot was on the *Hoi Ying:* we had come coasting into Seal, anchored behind Long Ledge, and settled down between two other hulls. At about two in the morning, there was a terrible crash of kitchenware someplace in the hull. I woke up feeling dizzy and disoriented, pried loose the foredeck hatch cover, and looked straight down over the side into water a few feet away. *Hoi Ying* was on her side, having lain down in a rising mudbank. I heard Bill Hazen, a friend of mine on the crew, start to get up below, and due to the angle, fall heavily to the cabin floor. He came up on deck white as a sheet, took one look at the situation,

and hissed hysterically, "Don't wake the girls. It'll scare them."

The irony of it was that when all of us, thoroughly awake, settled down to wait for the tide, we saw that the two other hulls, not a hundred feet to either side of us, continued to float undisturbedly vertical.

Back to our present cruise. I was taking dead reckoning data, jotting down the time of passing the buoys in a pencil log, noting the changes of course and changes of speed. This is not only a reassuring activity, but one with fairly practical application. If you miss your next mark, you still have a general idea of where you are.

We heard the Whitehead horn at this juncture. But I knew by my data that we were still a good way off and had no need to slow down. A mile and a half later, heading dead into the sound, suddenly—*Bloop! Blaahp!* —the blast was much louder and more peremptory. The time after that it blatted so harshly that it seemed as though we must be about to strike it. We emerged out of the milk white and saw solid rock. I swung the boat about and we followed the shore. We never did see the horn itself.

Leaving the noise of the horn behind, we plowed stolidly on into the tangle of Muscle Ridge, almost an act of faith in this fog. Our first mark was a can: this one had the number *1* on it. On our 1203 chart, this can was considerably inside our course. This was fortunately not another illustration of my faltering navigation that day, but an illustration of the usefulness of the large-scale chart. As soon as we got out our 310, it showed, as the small-scale 1203 did not, that there were *two* cans in the vicinity marked *1* and we were on course after all.

We pressed ahead blind: mark to mark, taking grateful cognizance of each as it glided toward us out of the milk curtain—Can 5 off High Clam Ledge, then the beacon on Otter Island Ledge, then Bell 11 off Ash

*New Harbor: breakfast in the cockpit*

*Map 9: Penobscot Bay*

1. SLIDE *course from Tenant's Harbor and Muscongus Bay.*

2. *Dix Harbor, Muscle Ridge. Passage to West Penobscot Bay.*

3. *Upper Muscle Ridge. Gateway to West Penobscot Bay.*

4. *Inner Rockland Harbor. A large city with available supplies.*

5. *Outer Rockland Harbor anchorage.*

6. *Rockport Harbor, West Penobscot Bay.*

7. *Camden Harbor. Under the Blue Hills; repairs, supplies. One of the most beautiful and useful ports in Maine.*

8. *Cradle Cove, Seven Hundred Acre Island, West Penobscot Bay.*

9. *Lincolnville Beach, southwestern corner of Ducktrap Harbor.*

10. *Ducktrap Harbor. Northern anchorage, West Penobscot Bay.*

11. *Seal Harbor, Islesboro Island, West Penobscot Bay.*

12. *Saturday Cove, West Penobscot Bay.*

13. *Bayside harbor, West Penobscot Bay.*

14. *Belfast, West Penobscot Bay. A large city with supplies.*

15. *Searsport. At the head of West Penobscot Bay.*

16. *Course to the Penobscot River, Bucksport, Winterport, and Bangor.*

17. *Course to North Haven's western shore, upper East Penobscot Bay, Cape Rosier, Castine, and Eggemoggin Reach.*

18. *West anchorage, Pulpit Harbor, North Haven. One of the most famous of the Maine gunkholes. Plenty of room, shelter.*

19. *East anchorage, Pulpit Harbor, North Haven.*

20. *Barred Island Harbor, East Penobscot Bay.*

21. *Islesboro Harbor, Islesboro Island.*

22. *Sabbathday Harbor, Islesboro Island.*

23. *Holbrook Harbor, Cape Rosier.*

24. *Smith Cove, Bagaduce River.*

25. *Castine. A city with supplies and Maine's Maritime Academy.*

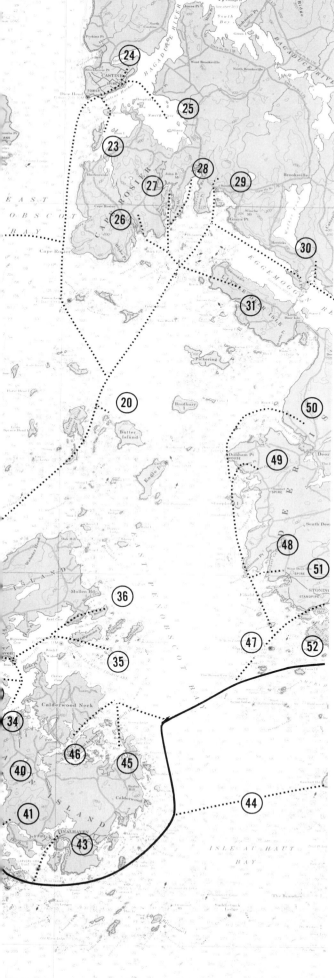

26. *Weir Cove, Cape Rosier.*

27. *Horseshoe Cove, Cape Rosier.*

28. *Orcutt Cove, Cape Rosier.*

29. *Buck Harbor, Eggemoggin Reach.*

30. *Billings Cove, Eggemoggin Reach.*

31. *Swains Cove, Little Deer Isle.*

32. *Fox Island Thorofare between North Haven Island and Vinalhaven Island.*

33. *Perry Cove anchorage, off Fox Island Thorofare, Vinalhaven Island.*

34. *Seal Cove, off Fox Island Thorofare, Vinalhaven Island.*

35. *Exit from Fox Island Thorofare to Lower East Penobscot Bay, going east toward the approaches to Mount Desert.*

36. *Little Thorofare. Passage going north and east out of Fox Island Thorofare toward upper East Penobscot Bay.*

37. SLIDE *course to Crockett's Cove and The Basin, Vinalhaven, West Penobscot Bay.*

38. *Crockett's Cove, Vinalhaven, West Penobscot Bay.*

39. *Long Cove, off Leadbetter Narrows.*

40. *The Basin, Vinalhaven. Landlocked interior harbor of the island, connected by narrow tide run to the bay.*

41. *Old Harbor, Vinalhaven.*

42. *Hurricane Island. Site of the Outward Bound boys' camp.*

43. *Carver's Harbor. The main port of Vinalhaven Island. A salty picturesque fishing harbor; the town is called Vinalhaven.*

44. *Course to Isle au Haut Thorofare, Isle au Haut Island.*

45. *Seal Bay, off Winter Harbor, Vinalhaven Island.*

46. *Winter Harbor, Vinalhaven. Long inland reach.*

47. *Course to south and west shores of Deer Isle.*

48. *Stonington, Deer Isle. A town with good supplies and lots of history; a boatbuilding and granite port.*

49. *Burnt Cove, Deer Isle, west shore.*

50. *Sylvester Cove, Deer Isle, west shore.*

51. *Northwest Cove, Deer Isle, west shore.*

52. SLIDE *course to Merchant's Row, Jericho Bay, and the approaches to Blue Hill Bay and Mount Desert (see Map Ten, page 130).*

This is a planning aid; use only U.S. Geodetic charts for navigation.

*New Harbor: getting the dinghy dry*

*Gunning out of Otter Island
harbor, headed for the Penobscot*

Island. We finally chugged up to Nun 2 in Owl's Head Channel and we were out of Muscle Ridge and practically home free. Bliss.

There is, while we are on the topic of marks, a good investment to be had for twenty-five cents, the little U.S. Oceanographic *Nautical Chart Symbols and Abbreviations* (send the money in stamps to Washington, D.C., if you haven't got a local chart store that carries it). The publication explains all the little squiggly and straight lines, asterisks, dots, underlines, colors, buoys, soundings on the charts. (For instance a sounding in slanted letters has a different meaning than a sounding marked in straight.) There are also some esoterics like coral reef, lava flow, oyster beds, and Shinto shrines. And what a symbol collector's day when you sail by a "levee"!

It was now, in Owl's Head Reach, about four thirty. Kim and Lorna were beginning to feel the effects of the long run in the fog (symptoms: listlessness, fatigue, indifference to death), so it was with a light-hearted

swerve that I finally turned *Puff* around the corner to Rockland.

We came in on the commercial marina float (the best place to come in) south of Crockett Point. This marina is the site of the great Maine Seafood Festival, an annual eatout which attracts tourists from all over. Out in back of the marina here were two giant tanks, proudly billed as the "World's Largest Lobster Kettles." The churches of the town lend their supper tables and everyone gets a belly full of lobster and clams out of the caldrons.

The Massies were walked to the Greyhound bus station in town and we picked up groceries and ice on the way back, loaded up, and headed for the farthest corner of the harbor to anchor for the night.

This is the northeast corner of Rockland Harbor, right in front of the Samoset Hotel. I had always had a yen to see the Samoset, which is a survival of an elegant era, so we took the dinghy, and with some tricky footwork, stepped ashore dry. We walked the dinghy, which Pat had named *X-ray,* up out of the way of the rising tide and climbed up the bank to the hotel. Samoset is Saratoga and Newport in one magnificent building. It is a high clapboard frame holding a set of huge picture windows that overlook svelte lawns sweeping down to Penobscot Bay. Gleaming fixtures, uniformed bellboys, soft carpets, and high ceilings: all overlaid with a hush of general well-being. We decided against having drinks and dinner here (need coat and tie, dress) and by seven were back on *Puff,* anchored in the fringe of lobster pots, starting dinner.

A lone lobster fisherman came by, chugging slowly up to us. "Got anything to cook with?" he asked. We said we did. He hauled a trap and presented us with a wriggling lobster. He would not take a beer or payment. I keep forgetting how much spontaneity there is up in Maine and am reminded of it when someone offers his car or makes a present of a lobster.

*The world's most beautiful bay: the Penobscot*

THURSDAY, AUGUST 18. Rockland will be remembered mostly for her past, the Maine Seafood Festival notwithstanding. It was here in Rockland that the great Maine clipper *Red Jacket* was built, the ship that still holds the sailing record, west–east on the Atlantic. Here also, in 1609, a small ship came in and let her crew ashore to cut a mast: Henry Hudson's ill-fated *Half Moon* was off for Hudson's Bay.

I consider Rockland and nearby Camden out of the way in terms of the SLIDE course (see Map Nine, page 116). However, Camden is something special and if you only have time for one side trip on your cruise, you might well make this the one.

The sun was barely over the breakwater of the Rockland harbor when we were skimming out the entrance and headed for Camden. The sun was gorgeous. The Penobscot lay like a summer heaven, all blue and faceted with exploding reflected glints from the sun that was burning down on this, the world's most beautiful bay. We were headed for an appointment in Camden with James Rockefeller, the owner of the Bald Mt. Boat Works, to talk about the Friendship sloops that he was making.

Camden is the beauty port of the Maine coast. It doesn't have the austere, cathedral impressiveness of Mount Desert's rock walls, but Camden is more than compensated by its famous Blue Hills: a series of hazily shimmering blue rock escarpments that show high over the city in all good weather. As we came in today, the rounded edges of cobalt and purple tracing through Camden's sky more than fulfilled our expectations.

The harbor was, as usual, alive with sail and power craft going in and coming out. It is one of the four big yachting centers of the coast (Falmouth Foreside, Boothbay, Camden, and Mount Desert). One-Designs were racing out to meet us, sleek hulls with classic long-ended bows and sterns rising and swooping with the swell. Chunky little Turnabouts were racing to our right as we came through the expensive lovely yachts of the moored power and sail fleet. Beyond that were the commercial docks for yachtsmen. We found a hole in the line of hulls at the Wayfarer Marine floats (float space is hard come by in Camden) and tied up. The dockhand who helped us allowed how more and more outboard cruisers were coming into Camden every year. (Outboards are the future, Maine marina owners, don't fight it.)

James Rockefeller turned out to be a friendly-eyed and soft-spoken man with a very precise and economical way of saying things. He has as his object to build Friendship sloops the way they used to be built. He has so far produced two spanking new ones to the old "*Pemaquid* pattern." The original *Pemaquid* was the fastest of the thirty-foot Friendships in her day and her successor Pemaquids may be still. (One of Rockefeller's designs took a second in the last Friendship annual.) We hopped into the Rockefeller car which already had two passengers—Ricky and Olive, two young college types. We were driven at great rapidity up toward the Bald Mountain Boat Works.

— Why did he build a boatyard on Bald Mountain?

— Because that's where he lives.

— Why did he decide to build Friendships?

— When you build Friendships, the whole State of Maine is behind you.

— What is the best rig for the hull?

— The Friendship is usually rigged with a big gaff main and a jib-foresail combination forward. With this rig she balances nicely on all points of sailing. And she is fast, carrying nearly twice the canvas of an ordinary twenty-eight- or thirty-footer.

— Why buy a Friendship?

— Everyone on the coast knows the design by sight. People come over and talk to you; it is a great way to get to meet people. Besides, it is one great boat to sail. It's a lot of boat.

— What does a Friendship Pemaquid from the Bald Mountain Boat Works cost?

— Ten to twelve thousand dollars.

We wound upward and upward past Lake Meguntic behind Camden, and we reached the peak of Bald Mountain, the place where James had bought an old farm and was in the process of completely restoring it. He had added to it a connecting section and a large building done in a modern Scandinavian style. The latter contained the Bald Mountain Boat Works. Inside, in the light of the late afternoon, an old Friendship with lovely swept hull lines was being restored, plank by plank. The hull belonged to a Portland man; since it was an original Wilbur Morse Friendship (Morse is one of three or four famous original builders of the workboat), the owner naturally was anxious to have her remain Morse's. Though she was replaced plank by plank and rib by rib, if her lines were absolutely intact he could still say with Down East conviction he had a Wilbur Morse.

Indeed she was beautiful. Her lines flowed back into the shed where two or three skilled shipwrights (a good shipwright is hard to come by these days) were bending a plank over the side of the hull. The shed was redolent of wood shavings, glue, and other good smells. You could get a feeling of how pleasant preassembly-line manual labor must have been, not only for shipwrights but for all. There was, in this shed, an air of simple peace, of men talking in easy tones to each other as they worked, of the measured competence and boundless confidence of men in control of a process. Possibly this explained the why of Bald Mountain Boat Works more than anything else. What more satisfying thing than to have re-created this world?

James had a real old-style office in solid paneling (no plywood) above the boat works and here we discussed shipbuilding. He proposed that rather than spend money trying to create ski areas in and around

*Inner harbor at Camden*

*Fishing vessel in the Penobscot*

the coast (as the Federal Government has done here and there), a more auspicious path would be to re-create a small part of the famous Maine sailing ship industry, modeled after the typical yards of the 1700s. A little seed money could start a yard or two in Maine building classic workboats, up to and including the old-time Maine schooners. In the long run, markets would eventually be created and we might see lots of small yards come alive in Maine, building pleasure boats.

To take the matter a little further, as we did that afternoon, why not have a couple of these yards as the centrum for a Maine version of Connecticut's Mystic seaport? James said that he had thought about just such a thing, and that he had a place picked that would be perfect. The "Maine Seaport" would preserve not only the skills but the few schooners that are still left from the old days—and perhaps re-create one or two of the most famous schooners of Maine's history. Nothing is as perishable as a yacht or ship once the interest in keeping her up is gone.

After our talk, we met James's wife Liv, Norwegian-born, and we had a quick look at the house filled with Norwegian furniture and hangings whose richness mated excellently with the simple lines of the Yankee rooms. There must have been, on this evidence, something close and kindred in Maine to the spirit of the old Vikings on their beloved and intricate coast. Liv probably hit it when she explained why she had not liked living in the American South. "It is all so flat. There are no surprises around the corner," she said.

There was still fine sunlight on the harbor at five thirty as we backed *Puff* off the float. We motored slowly out toward the Penobscot as it lay blinking beyond the lighthouse; I was reminded of another departure that I had made from Camden a few years back. It had been in the *Talaria,* a big three-masted Herreshoff schooner. A crew of us had been at anchor between a couple of cruise ships, the *Mattie* and the

*Mercantile;* the latter were filled to the brim with schoolmarms and city types out for a Maine cruise. I had Bill Hazen aboard again. Bill had acted as the navigator for the earlier *Hoi Ying* cruise, but had flatly refused to do it again: too much strain, he said. Now, as we made sail, Hazen dived below and came back up on deck clad in his full Lieutenant's (jg) Navy dress summer uniform. As the rest of us struggled to man the lines and swing our yacht by the *Mattie* and its railful of admiring females, Bill, standing on the near side with his hands negligently in his jacket pockets turned his head slightly aft and snapped, "O.K. men, take her out!" It's moments like that you can't take away from a man.

Outside Camden, we headed for Pulpit Harbor on North Haven, the big island in the center of the Penobscot, where we would overnight. A stiff chop had set in, our first real waves since the big gale off Cape Porpoise. *Puff* was soon throwing out great satisfying white wings of spray, her bow regally in the air, disdaining to let her decks get wet. I decided to take the dinghy aboard to give us a bit more speed. Pat took the helm and slowed the hull while I started to haul *X-ray* up on the fore-deck.

The trouble hit.

I had *X-ray* halfway up when my heel slipped. In and under went your author. It was only tragic in that I had a pair of specially wrought, forty-dollar, prescription-ground sunglasses on my head. They were tied around with a string, it's true, but with the force of the plunge, they slipped off and went gleaming into the depths.

My temper was only fractionally restored by the heady toss and surge of the waves and the fan of the bow spray against the setting sun as we went for Pulpit. On such a day as this, I thought, did Martin Pring, doughty English explorer, come toward these islands in the middle of the Penobscot in 1603 and name them

Fox Islands for all the rich-pelted gray fox that ran so freely along the shores. Cheered by immersion in history, I started taking some pictures.

As we approached North Haven's shore, we could see the "low" in the trees and then the mastheads of the yachts inside Pulpit sticking up over Pulpit Rock, the huge singular rock formation which guards the entrance. I dived below and reloaded my Leica, thinking to get this particular shot for my collection. When I got back up, Pat had put the boat dead for the opening south of Pulpit Rock and we were almost in it. It had been several years since I'd been here: I had a moment of indecision. We could probably sneak over the bar south of the rock rather than go around north of it, could we not? Half my mind was on picture taking, which shows the folly of combining roles. The Raytheon quickly set me right, flicking to five feet, four feet . . . "Stop," I said loudly. "Back her up, quick." It wasn't quite quick enough. In spite of the reversed engines, *Puff* drifted onto the bar with a grinding sound as I shouted, "Shut them down!" I went over the side in a quick crabwise motion, got my feet on the rocky bottom, and performed "manual backing." One powerboat and one lobster boat, thinking to help, had started out of the harbor (we were in full view of six to eight yachts anchored inside), but I at least got *Puff* off and and was back aboard before they were close enough to offer help. Naturally, the dinghy line got tangled in the propeller housings, so *that* had to be cleared up by vigorous strokes with the boathook. Then we powered off with the casual air of having just gone in to look for a few clam beds.

We went around to the north of the rock then and came in properly through the deep channel where the fathometer read a reassuring 60, 50, 40, instead of 6, 5, and 4. We swung into the southern fork of Pulpit. Here there were fewer yachts moored and none who had seen our *faux pas*. Since it was low tide I put the anchor down in ten feet of water and let out enough line to give us five-to-one scope at high tide. In a less roomy situation, we could have done with less scope, and would have anchored in somewhat shallower water to reduce the overall length of the line.

Dinner. Baked beans and frankfurters over the charcoal grill. Cucumber salad, canned potatoes, pears for dessert. Coffee. Peace.

Evening slid slowly over the harbor. The marvelous last hours of the evening were disturbed only fitfully by the thought that the day had seen me commit the two most egregious errors of a sailor: falling overboard and running aground.

*Friday, August 19.* This morning we lallygagged around on deck. As Water Rat says in *The Wind in the Willows*, "There is nothing, absolutely nothing half so much worth doing as simply messing about in boats." *The Wind in the Willows* is now passé as a children's book, I suppose, but very few books used to be written on boating without using Rat's quote and I am going to stay within the rule. What some quoters of Rat's words don't know, perhaps, is that in the next instant after his deathless line, Rat runs his craft into the bank of the river.

A rough log is the cryptic account kept underway provided nothing serious threatens: mine reads for this day, "Lv Pulpit, North Haven, 12:10."

In inimitable prose, it continues: "Weather early bright, later graying a bit. Slack wind outside. Flat on W. Penobscot. Top speed 17."

This is a rather penurious description of the sensation of coasting along on the top layer of the extraordinary and gigantic bowl of blue in the West Penobscot, with the undulant smoking beauty of the hills behind Camden to one side and the long, running lie of North Haven to the other. A single sailboat motored down far, far behind us, seemingly a thousand miles off on hazy

blue water which was disturbed only here and there by a ripple from a wandering zephyr. Overhead, cumulus and flatter clouds plied through a sky as calm as the sea. One savors moments, and minutes, such as these because it is truly what one comes to Maine to have.

We were moving down toward Leadbetter Narrows to rejoin the SLIDE course off Vinalhaven, the southernmost of these two huge islands in the middle of the Penobscot. Vinalhaven's shores, for my money, have by far the most fascinating inlets and harbors on any comparable stretch of coast.

By choice, we were leaving behind the whole upper part of the West Penobscot, where lie such storied harbors and islands and towns that it is enough to make one swear to return some other summer. The Penobscot River runs in at the top of the West Penobscot, and that is navigable all the way up to Bangor. Have a look at Map Nine, page 116, and you'll get an idea of what you have available. It includes a run down Eggemoggin Reach, one of the very nicest stretches on the coast. We left this and we also bypassed Fox Island Thorofare, between the two big islands; I simply find the southern

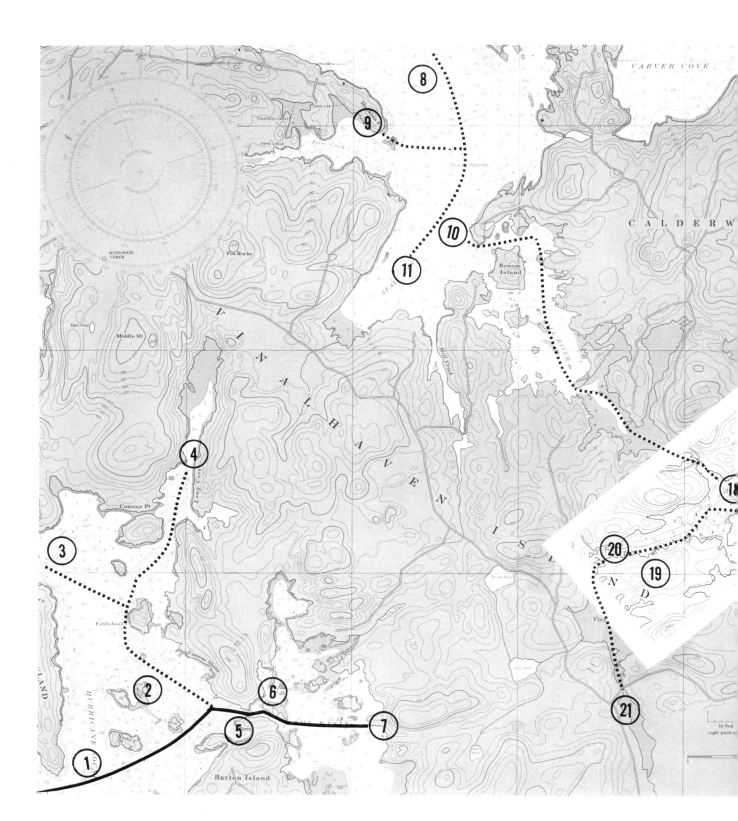

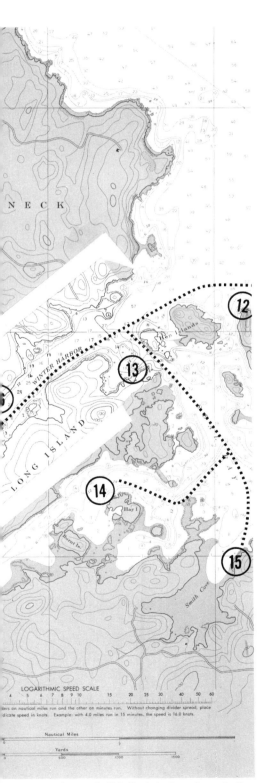

Map 10: Vinalhaven Island

1. SLIDE course from Muscle Ridge and
   West Penobscot Bay.

2. Course to deep-water anchorages and
   Leadbetter Narrows.

3. Long Cove, Vinalhaven Island.

4. Course to Crockett's Cove, Vinalhaven Island.

5. Upper Tide Falls. Entrance to The Basin.

6. Lower Tide Falls. Entrance to The Basin.

7. Eastern anchorage, The Basin.

8. Course from Fox Island Thorofare.

9. Perry Cove, Vinalhaven, off Fox Island Thorofare.

10. Seal Cove, Vinalhaven. Dinghy route: through the
    island to Winter Harbor.

11. Seal Cove anchorage.

12. Course from East Penobscot Bay into
    outer Winter Harbor.

13. Course to Seal Bay, Vinalhaven, off Winter Harbor.

14. Smith Cove, off Seal Bay.

15. Hay Island anchorage, off Seal Bay.

16. Starboard Rock at the entrance to
    Inner Winter Harbor.

17. Starboard Rock Creek.

18. Tidal stream. End of dinghy route from Seal Cove.

19. Inner Winter Harbor. Old quarry at water's edge.

20. Head of Navigation, Inner Winter Harbor. Under
    old marble quarry derrick.

21. Head of Vinal Cove. A dinghy run from
    Inner Winter Harbor.

a planning aid; use only U.S. Geodetic charts for navigation.

*Negotiating the tricky channel
leading into The Basin,
Vinalhaven Island*

shore of Vinalhaven more interesting.

About twelve thirty as we headed for Leadbetter Narrows we saw an enormous three-masted gaff-rigged schooner come regally from the direction of Fox Island Thorofare. I knew at once that we'd come across *Victory Chimes,* a cruise boat famous on the coast, the last three-masted Maine schooner in existence. She seemed at least three hundred feet long although she goes under half of that. She was under motor and sail, and the dark green cast to her hull seemed to make her loom up like Admiral Nelson's *Victory.* One expected *at least* Admiral Nelson in epaulettes and braid to lean over the rail and halloo, "Wha-a-t shi-i-p?" before opening the gunports. *Victory Chimes* had instead a jolly bear of a captain waving both hands aloft at friends in various cottages along the shore as we trailed her into Leadbetter. A row of summer-cruising types aboard, male and female, were shooting pictures of us as I shot pictures of them—and that was the extent of the exchange of fire. We let *Victory Chimes* go, glad she has had a kinder fate than has met the thousand other giants of the Maine coast in the past hundred years, giants that now exist as at most a rotten rib or two sticking above water as a final memorial to an era and a coast whose mores and hardihoods filtered into the language and thinking of the whole young nation. ("How stands the Union?" "Rock-ribbed and copper-sheathed, sir!")

Our destination was that great, secluded, nearly landlocked bay called simply The Basin. It is a bay connected by a narrow tidal passage to the sea. Duncan and Blanchard warns flatly against going in here because of the narrowness of the passage, but at the risk of being accused of overmuch sangfroid, I will say that it is not an unusually difficult passage if you hit it at high slack, a time of the day that comes a bit *after* high slack as registered in the tide tables for the town of Vinalhaven. Any yacht carrying five feet or less that

waits until the tide is high slack in the passage can make it through with circumspect navigation. The only thing is, unless one has lots of power, one may have to wait twelve hours or so for the next high slack in order to make one's way out; however, with the outboard rig and kick-up motors such as our Evinrudes (they come up if they hit anything underwater), I should say you could go in with the tide anytime; also out anytime except at the very strongest of the incoming tide.

However, if you have doubts about the idea, anchor outside first and take the dinghy in. If you still should decide that you want to skip it, go on to the very cozy Crockett's Cove just north of Leadbetter for the night.

Best time to hit, as I have said, is when the tide outside is somewhat *after* official slack high tide (which lasts about an hour here); this gives you the advantage of eight to ten feet over the depths marked on the chart. (See Map Ten, page 130.)

We took the entrance at 1 P.M. which according to the U.S. Coast and Geodetic Survey Tide Tables should have been just after high slack. But it takes a while to fill The Basin from the outside through this narrow gut. We could see in the gut a regular torrent of white water pouring through. Since I was impatient to get in, I took the motors back to idle and let the hull suck into the stream, something I'd normally think twice about doing. So I thought twice and I did it.

We bounced down the overfall at a fine clip; I scanned anxiously for smooth "tongues of water" which, as my canoeing has taught me, usually indicate the deeper passage in a stream. The first narrows, south of the single rock in the entrance, was easy; it is only on the order of thirty-five or so feet wide (I noted quickly) and you pretty much *had* to shoot it dead center, no choice. And that went fine. But the second overfall, in spite of being a wider spot, has a much bigger drop and several nasty eddies. The effect of each eddy was to give the stern a sharp jerk forward and set us on the bias to the current. This had to be immediately countered by a shove on the throttle and a twist of the wheel to straighten us out and keep us pointed down the stream. And even though the water was deeper on the right, going in, I spotted a couple of rocks just below water there (you can see them if you watch for them), so I stayed in the center, approximately, all the way until I could see the relatively large, flat-topped rock that marks the northern boundary of the exit into The Basin (it is the largest of the final rocks).

Coming into The Basin was like being shot from the hurly-burly world into the Peaceable Kingdom. If you were lifted bodily, vessel and all, into a small lake about a mile and a half long and a mile wide in the middle of Maine, you wouldn't be more sheltered or surrounded by quiet. Of course, just as in inland Maine, there is liable to be a boat or two on the lake but, largely, you are away from people and noise. (Because of the time factor involved in hitting slack tide, not many cruising vessels stay in here, although a good number of them may come in on the slack and coast about and then leave again before the tide starts to run again.)

At the high cliff at the far side, a couple of really spectacular two-story granite boulders made a great backdrop (aesthetics is important in cruising) to the scene. We tied to the low gnarled branches of a stumpy bayberry bush here and heaved a stern anchor out to keep the boat from drifting too near the rock. It was now high tide. By evening, I would know how much to shorten the stern anchor line to keep the bow off the rock all night.

What do you do in The Basin?

Well, on a sunny day, you just enjoy it. There was a small breeze riffling our "lake" and the sunlight was bouncing gloriously off the wall of granite, reflecting into the cockpit like a welcome fire. It was warm. In fact, for the first time on the cruise, it was really *hot*.

I got up on the handiest shelf of the boulders and did an eight-foot dive into the cool fifty-foot-deep dark blue water. It was bracing but certainly not uncomfortable. And then I dried out on the warm bosom of the rock. And napped perchance.

Toward dusk, we spotted a lobster fisherman pulling in traps and we waved him over. He was a gentle-spoken man, as most of the lobster fishermen seem to be, young or old. He'd be delighted to sell us a couple he'd just liberated from the traps and pegged. You can pick unpegged lobster up with a grip across the back but keep it away from you. A lobster fisherman once told me that if a lobster gets a claw on you, either dunk it in water or step on it. In either case, it will relax the claw. Otherwise he will *hurt* you.

Lobster has to be steam-cooked until red, and on an alcohol stove, this takes a bit of doing. Not too much water, about enough to half cover the shell, or it takes too long to do. Then turn them once in a while. After half an hour or so in steaming water—ah, that is *fresh* lobster.

Lobster has been called almost everything from heavenly to a nasty mess; it is indubitably one of the world's really distinctive foods. The animal has been around the Atlantic coast in pretty much the same form as you see it now for 100 million years and that is more than man can say. Of course, we have overtaken the lobster somewhat in development but we can still extravagantly admire its content. Figures indicate that lobster bring 50 million dollars a season to the fishermen, who catch 70 million of them from North Carolina to Newfoundland every year. (The biggest lobster on record is the 42-pounder in the Boston Museum of Natural History; it is 3 feet 5½ inches long.) The lobster starts life as a little lobsterbit hung in an egg on the underside of its mother for nearly a year with some 65,000 brethren. When it hatches, it falls off and starts to grow, eating plankton and shedding its shell

eight times in the first year, five in the second, and three times in the third. After that the lobster sheds once a year in summer. Its shell cracks along the back and it jackknifes out. If it's lost a foot or a claw, a replacement grows while the lobster is waiting for its new shell to harden. By the time a new shell forms, it's 15 percent longer and perhaps half again as heavy as it was before. By the time it's five years old, it's a one-pound "chicken" lobster and probably the most succulent size for eating. (Big lobster are not usually as tender.)

If you're buying lobster on your cruise, you avoid the "shedder," or lobster about to leave its shell. There's little meat inside and the shell itself feels thin and bendable, rather than hard and firm.

*Saturday, August 20.* This turned out to be another fantastic blue-sky day. We woke to the gentle rocking of the boat and the reveille tattoo of small wavelets on the hull. The overfall on the far side was "turned on" and it made a comforting rushing noise, like a stream past a cabin door. We had the delicious feeling of no hurry. What more could one ask than to tether securely to a Maine rock and wait for the sun to light up The Basin?

The small wood shack perched on the boulder above was part of the scene. I for my part had no desire to look into it. This was someone else's vacation home. I had mine. The morning round of gull talk began. One gull cries and another answers piercingly, plaintively, as quickly as possible. The first replies almost instantaneously. There is soon a cacaphonous counterpoint going; one gull misses the turn and then it stops briefly, only to have another pair or the same pair take it up again, circling all the while. Sometimes one gull tries to sing both parts by itself, but it soon shuts up for lack of encouragement.

I was feeling particularly brave this morning be-

cause of my previous success in coming in through the gut so smoothly; I decided to see if the equipment could or could not take the full force of the current. I figured that the fastest current would be at the maximum difference in levels inside and outside and that ought to come between twelve and twelve thirty, just before the rate of rise in the water outside slowed toward high slack. Just for insurance, I decided to try it at eleven rather than at the time of the *very* fastest current. So I deposited Pat on the rock north of the inside entrance (you can park your bow on the inner end of this without any problem) to have her snap pictures of the Great Ascent Over the Inner Overfall.

I came into the white water slowly, not knowing whether I needed to go at a run or not. The game is to hold the bow dead into the current so that one doesn't get turned sidewise to it and get washed back like a dead leaf. As I got to the first tongues of clear water between the white standing waves, I slowly pushed the throttle forward and found I didn't need quite full to move upstream. All in all, the inner fall is about a hundred feet long, I'd say. By the middle, the boat's bow was trying to turn this way and that like a wayward mount, and I upped it to almost full throttle to keep going. *Puff* steadied and up she went to the brink at the top; here she needed just a bit more persuasion to go over. Now I was in fairly shallow water, probably five feet, looking down through clear water at the sorcerous-looking green waving weeds on the dark rocks.

I now swung her around and danced carefully back down to where Pat was waiting, took her aboard, and back up we went. This time it was a bit harder. The strength of the inner fall had increased measurably and I had Pat's weight aboard. We wavered halfway up and I put on full power, thinking to jump us to the top. Instead, *Puff* had to fight her way slowly up the watery incline. At the top an eddy turned her sharply

and caused the propellers to cavitate (spin without biting). I had to wrench her around to the left abruptly and as soon as the props hit less turbulence, they bit in and pushed up—rather slowly for my taste—over the brink. From there on out, it was a piece of cake.

Our next stop was a side trip.

We were going for Hurricane Island where there is one of this country's several Outward Bound schools —HIOBS or Hurricane Island Outward Bound School. This is an outgrowth of a seamen's survival school set up in England during the war and later copied in the extracurricular program of Gordonstoun School, a boys' school in England.

The original seamen's school was set up to combat loss of life in World War II U-boat sinkings. Lawrence Holt, head of the Blue Funnel Lines, noted that, in the life-loss statistics on the sinkings, a lot of younger fitter men were drowning while older men with less strength were surviving. He got hold of Dr. Kurt Hahn, head of the Gordonstoun School (a fairly exclusive prep school Prince Charles later attended). Together Hahn and Holt set up the Aberdovy Sea School in Wales; they devised exercises and excitements to train the fledgling seaman to *think* survival and *believe* survival. Besides reducing casualties, the program had a really bracing moral effect on the seamen; Dr. Hahn incorporated it into Gordonstoun's athletic program. Graduates of the school and teachers involved in the program set up similar schools in Europe. In 1962 John Miner, now on the Phillips Exeter faculty, formerly of the faculty of Gordonstoun School, established the first Outward Bound school in the United States in Colorado. Two more were founded later. One is in Minnesota's wilderness lake country and the latest on Hurricane Island.

So much I knew by having looked at an advance folder (I got it by writing to Outward Bound, Inc., 16 School Street, Andover, Massachusetts), and now I was eager to see the theory in operation.

Hurricane is a handsome island among handsome islands here, its jutty granite shores jauntily set with evergreen. The buildings of HIOBS are easily apparent when one comes in from the north. They sit on the shore that faces northeast and there are a considerable number of huts and tents and a couple of magnificent tall timbered buildings that obviously are the showplaces. As we closed in, the HIOBS "fleet"—pulling boats (lifeboat types), sailcraft, and rescue cutters— lay between us and the float.

One of our greeters was "Mac" MacDonald, a teacher, and the other was Dr. Solvesen, the program's physician, an M.D., and a child psychologist to boot. Both were in their thirties.

They kindly took the time to explain the twenty-six-day program. Half the boys on the island pay $350 for the twenty-six days, and the other half pay nothing, coming from definitely disadvantaged backgrounds; quite a few of the latter are on their way to being, or are already, delinquents. The HIOBS training includes an elementary swim course called "drownproofing," a good deal of high- and low-rope walking, sailing, rowing, and "initiative" tests. As an example of the latter, the recruits are divided into "watches," and each twelve-man watch gets such problems as getting the entire watch over a twelve-foot timber wall. The Outward Bound idea is double-barreled: cooperation and individual initiative. Or, in the language of the school, compassion and survival.

The test of the survival training is when a boy is marooned on a small island and has to get along with a few matches, a mess tin, a small stove, and his wits. That is all he has for three days and three nights.

The most strenuous of the cooperative ventures is a four-day, 100-mile cruise in the pulling boats (which are equipped with sail). On this one, an instructor's powerboat stands off and oversees that the particular watch doesn't go hog-wild and decide to sail for

Carvers Harbor, Vinalhaven town:
a fisherman under steadying
sail puts in to the fish wharf

England.

I asked Dr. Solveson if he thought that this kind of school did kids with mental problems any kind of good.

"If they are ready for it," he said. "I wouldn't send any of my patients here right off, but if they have gotten to the point where they can distinguish fact from fantasy pretty well, then I'd say they could get a great deal out of it. On the other hand, if they can't, it could hurt them."

MacDonald mentioned that one of the boys, who was not ready, had shouted and screamed for a whole day on being marooned; they finally took him off.

After lunch, we went out to the quarry to watch drownproofing and mountain climbing. The drownproofing was the second lesson. They were going to try to float for thirty minutes. When we remembered that some of these kids, aged sixteen to twenty-two, had not swum at all before the first lesson, we found it a pretty impressive demonstration of the efficacy of this technique of "minimal swimming." Some of the pupils were well on their way to the half-hour goal when we left. This trial, successfully passed, gets them 10 points toward the perfect 100 for the twenty-six days at the school.

To get to the climbers, we walked a well-trodden path behind the quarry up to the top lip. Once up, we were rewarded by a superlative view of Penobscot Bay. The shadow of Matinicus stood out near the horizon, and inward the bay was blue, shot through with gems of reflected sun, setting in the rose and brown granite of the smooth wind-polished outlines of the islets. Far out in the bay, one of the pulling boats was maneuvering under double fore-and-aft sails, a tiny flake making toward the bronze and baize shores of Green Island.

The climbers were learning to belay single climbers up a face that, while short, still had the feeling of airiness, being high above the sea. The director of HIOBS, Peter O. Willauer, who was standing by watching, said,

"If a boy has difficulty tying a bowline at night on a boat . . . he will learn instantaneously on top of a cliff when he must tie his safety line with a bowline." The kingpin of the Outward Bound movement in the United States, Joshua Miner, was also standing by. I asked him how he had gotten the Outward Bound thing started over here. He said that when he had come back from Gordonstoun "no one was interested in the Outward Bound idea here, much less in contributing to setting up a school. But after Kennedy's inaugural address, things started breaking right and left."

The school, which has had some initial success in getting its graduates to be a more thoughtful bunch of young men, is still in a formative stage. The people there are the first to admit this. They probably need either a really first-class screening process—there's no sense having a boy come up to the island to produce repeated failures— or a very organized way of handling those who really can't take it.

HIOBS welcomes people interested in their idea. Provided you are content to watch and do not insist on taking up too much time in the very busy lives of the people who run the program on Hurricane, you can stay to watch what is going on. And don't forget to climb the quarry trail. The view is the best.

I now carefully laid out courses and wrote bearings for the next two stops: Vinalhaven, the "capital" of the island, and then east to Winter Harbor, a marvelous landfall way up a "tidal fjord."

The game of laying courses is one of the most amusing and important among the skills of cruising. It is de rigueur to spend the time necessary to do this for your complete day's run before you take off. Much time can be wasted by failing to lay compass courses to run; once you miss a course and move aimlessly around, you will see that.

There are several ways to go about course laying. One way is to start with the destination and work back-

Lord Jim: *this is what is meant by a "gold plater"*

wards, avoiding the rocks and bad passages and keeping to recognizable marks as much as possible. This system, if there were a buoy every few hundred yards along the route, would be simple. You'd draw courses from buoy to buoy. But there are lots of places without buoys where you want to make a turn and need to know exactly where the turn is: this kind of certainty allows you to pass *between* unbuoyed ledges and rocks, rather than *over* them.

One solution is to turn on an "abeam bearing." You pick one end of an island or a rock which shows at high tide and make your turn when the point in question is abeam or exactly at right angles to the boat. While it might be difficult to ascertain when an object has a bearing of say fifty degrees off the boat's course, it is pretty easy to tell when you have an object at right angles to the course: your eye is used to "square corners" as an experience of everyday living. The point defined by the meeting of your course and the line at right angles to it can be used as a definite point to turn on, just as can the point defined by a buoy.

Proceeding from Hurricane, we left the far island of Matinicus off our starboard beam. (For a rundown on this island see our return voyage in the last chapter.) We turned on buoys and abeam bearings so that we brought *Puff* handily into Carver's Harbor where lies the fishing village of Vinalhaven. Advice: take special care to avoid a rock which lies right on the course from buoy to buoy on the way in; look at the inset of U.S. chart 310: it will be just at the entrance to the inner harbor. (Incidentally, the little figure in parentheses beside a rock marked on the chart does not represent a depth, but the height of the rock above water at low tide. If there is no figure next to it, but a dotted circle around it, the presumption is that it just breaks water, or is a foot or so out, or a foot or two under, at low tide. These latter are the dillies, the ones that hardly ever show themselves.)

Going into the harbor, there is a Gulf wharf at the left, where we tied up; next to it is the dock where the Vinalhaven fleet's catch is brought in and where, consequently, you can get crushed ice for the refrigerator.

I find the lobster fisherman plying his trade alone somehow more simpatico and bone-honest than the rougher men who go to sea in fishing smacks, but I am glad that Vinalhaven is still the active fishing port that it is. The saltiest talk on the coast bounces out over the water from any group of fishermen lounging about on the piers.

We shopped a bit in the town of Vinalhaven itself, a ten-minute walk from the Gulf wharf. I found that it was not a particularly attractive town compared to Camden, say. There were too many cars zipping through, and the people seemed in a rush, out of character with a Maine coast town as I'd like to see it. But there were plenty of supplies and we came back with everything we'd gone for.

When we came back an eighty-foot schooner, *Lord Jim,* was tied at the front of the pier, completely dwarfing *Puff*. The schooner was a picture: polished brightwork, clipper bowsprit, ladder stays; it looked like it had sailed out of a wide-screen production.

She took off before we did; I had the satisfaction of seeing her professional captain head out along the buoys and then suddenly remember The Rock. He veered off his course and took a new one farther out to his right and didn't turn until he had an abeam bearing on Nun 2 off Norton Point, which was the same point I had picked out as an abeam turning point. "Even the good ones sometimes have lapses," I whispered comfortingly to myself.

Now we ran up behind *Lord Jim* and left her in our wake, a lean fast sprinter leaving the heavy leviathan behind. We rounded Vinalhaven and ran up the East shore toward the blue height of Bluff Head at the entrance to Winter Harbor. We were making good time.

We now lined into Winter Harbor, a masterfully contrived cut going a long way into the East Coast of Vinalhaven. (See Map Ten, page 130.)

"The Bible" has an account by a skipper who has navigated to the end of normally navigable water here in Winter Harbor, but it is somewhat out of date due to the disappearance of a fish weir he relies on as a mark. But I had other directions from Pete Rand; by combining this with Coast and Geodetic Survey Chart 235, we got in easily. The high arch of Starboard Rock lies at the beginning of the "difficulties"; we were at low tide so I could see the outline of the channel pretty well. The still-standing tripod of the old granite quarry derrick stands at the head of navigable water at Winter Harbor to mark the anchorage.

We had motored slowly in toward the derrick, reading ten feet almost all the way except for a few aberrant moments when I wandered out of the channel while looking up at the walls and hills of the harbor. We puttered up the narrowest neck of the harbor past the solid pier of granite block on which the derrick stood, and found only five feet or less off it. We went back below the derrick again until I had ten feet in midstream and a much wider space to swing in.

This was prime granite quarrying territory. Undoubtedly millions of pounds of Maine's proud rock has gone into the holds of the granite barges here. In the evening light, the silhouette of the derrick showed that some thoughtful osprey had made a nest atop it.

Anchor down, fires lit, the whispering rush of the small tide falls farther up the stream, and the day ended.

*A-boats race off Mt. Desert*

SUNDAY, AUGUST 21. A hot blue day. We blissfully agreed, before going on toward Mount Desert, to lay over at Winter Harbor for no other purpose than that of catching a hell of a tan. As we had our breakfast in the sun, white patches drifted by our hull lying under the old derrick; the tide fall up the passage had just reversed itself and foam was coming at us with the tide. We had the premier position at the head of the harbor, and no yacht could block the view of the white simmering stretch of falls unless it anchored precariously, up in the narrow neck. When the fall stopped bubbling, it was so quiet in Winter Harbor that I several times heard a sea gull land softly on the shallows.

An auxiliary yawl came in about ten in the morning; it motored up beside us. The crew smiled as they rode by. One said, "Hard to get anyplace first, isn't it?" And the yacht turned and circled back. A small playpen was tucked between the mizzen and the cockpit. I almost wished that they *had* been first. Much as I take little pleasure in the thought that the Maine coast is about to be inundated by a swarm of outboard, inboard, and auxiliary cruisers, and while it is true that old reliables like Pulpit Harbor are likely to be fairly full and it is true that it is hard to find float space in Boothbay, Camden, and Southwest, there are still harbors enough on the coast for many more hulls, even counting one harbor to a hull. Maine can use the money and its coast has plenty of room in that 2,500 miles.

The tide had now come in on the rock shores and covered the massy gold of its sea growth. We decided to take a walk before lunch and launched *X-ray*. We took her up a long flat stretch of rock to the southeast. Our goal was to walk across to Seal Bay on the other side of the height of land above us.

An old granite quarry opened up a few feet in from the sea as we landed. Salt water was pouring into the picturesque little quarry from an underground breach; it looked like a big swimming pool, but there was a mud bottom, so it was not fit for bathing.

We set off inland along one of a number of paths behind the quarry. At the entrance to this path, however, we were blocked by a blue spinnaker bag and a note on it which said "Be careful . . ." and then something undecipherable. We left it alone.

The path wound up out of the woods to an inland height with a bald rock cap. Here there were all kinds of Boy Scout path-marks—small rocks piled two and three high and rocks laid out in the form of arrows. We followed them in the perfection of the Maine midsummer day, with the scent of warm grass streaming to us and replacing—delightfully—the sea smells.

Along the route were articles of clothing—pants, T-shirts—hung on bushes and branches; I wondered if we'd stumbled into a mystery. What was it? Would we come upon wild revels of a secret society, prancing around a Maypole as they did in Roger Williams' Rhode Island? We walked across the top of the hill and then downhill until we hit water again. The arm of Seal Bay lay blue and green in the shallows. We sat on the edge of a pine woods and watched the shifting colors of the arm for a while. Then we left. On our way back we took a set of paths skirting the top of the hill and found a half-acre of wild huckleberry. We picked enough of the big black bits to have a tongue-tingling juicy appetizer.

When we got back to the quarry, we lay on its fine flat warm rocks for a while. After an hour or so of tanning, two little girls appeared and informed us that their family, summer people, were en route to this spot for a picnic. We thanked them and found that the girls were able to explain the note and the clothes. Their grandfather had put in here with a sailboat last night and left some clothes the family had wanted. The note was for them. As for the derelict clothing on the bushes, it had been strung to keep the gulls away from the huckleberries.

*Pat, musseling in Winter Harbor*

In the afternoon, we decided to explore the tidal falls above us and the shallow arm beyond. We rowed *X-ray* up the tidal run at high slack. The passage ran west and then turned south into quite a large lake, Vinal Cove. It seemed obvious that at high tide one could come in here comfortably, with a four- or five-foot draft and if one wanted to, anchor in the lake and wait for it to shrink down to a small pond with four or five feet of water in the middle and still be afloat when high tide came back twelve hours later. Good idea in a hurricane, anyway.

At high slack Vinal Cove was a small lake with pines on small islands, with cottages around the sides and a farm at the upper end. We rowed to a ledge near the border of the farm. The rock was just the right height for diving from and so we tried it. The water doesn't get much warmer on the Maine coast than we had it right here; it is not terribly warm, but refreshing. We rowed back down the passage, drying in the sun.

Back aboard, we spotted a blue motor cruiser moving up toward us. It prospected about in the bay of which we occupied the upper anchorage and, seemingly unsatisfied, came up to talk. "Have you been here awhile?" Yes, we said, we had. (We were old-timers at Winter Harbor now.) "Seen any bricks above water at low tide?" We said we had seen ledges farther down the harbor but none up here. "Thanks," the owner said. "Got a few scattered blips on my fathometer here which usually means there are some bricks down there." He motored off and anchored two hundred feet down from us.

He was certainly a very pleasant fellow and he had a nice wife and children with him. Yet I took umbrage at "bricks." Rocks is a perfectly good word. If I'd taken him literally . . . in my mind's eye, I saw his hull tilting crazily at low tide, hung on a stalagmite of a rock. Bricks, no, mister; only that big rock you're hung on.

He had a big boat, with a big living room on deck and a radar screen on top. Was I envious? After all, I had a boat that was light and airy and tight as a drum in a rainstorm and a minimum investment and a minimum of trouble. Would I want another ten feet of boat? You bet.

The evening sky looked a bit gray. The faithful WHDH marine weather report stated that we would have clouds and possible rain with the wind swinging northeast tomorrow. (This is about the worst direction wind can take, and holds out little promise of clear weather.) Pat put some magic into our dinner of canned hash and tinned green string beans that S. S. Pierce never put there, but she wasn't satisfied. She said we ought to have fresh groceries in the morning.

"This isn't a grocery cruise, lass," I intoned sternly.

Women can get out of hand if allowed to believe that each day will include a stop at a nearby market whenever the ship runs out of fresh lettuce. Possibly this inclination is a nervous reflex to being trapped in a rather masculine world; it is possibly a manifest reminder to males that the cook does, after all, fuel the captain and crew. I find that the reflex will, however, subside under stern repression.

*Monday, August 22.* This morning had a perceptible temperature drop to it and intermittent rain. Forecast was for more of same. We thought we'd see if it would clear a bit before we went for our next goal: Mount Desert, the next to last section of our SLIDE cruise. Right after breakfast, Pat put on foul weather gear and took off for the mussel beds. Low tide was at nine thirty: she was going to steam us mussels for lunch. Musseling around the shelves of the quarry, she got a goodly bunch. The wild Maine mussel is not the neat shiny mussel of Mussels Polipso or Mussels Marinara in your New York restaurant. In natural state they cling in tight little scrambled colonies consisting of big mussels, little mussels, seaweed, snails, pebbles, and plain tidal mud. It is a mixed bag meshed in a woolly tangle of weed.

The reason for the mélange is that mussels coexist in colonies, each mussel taking a firm bite on a piece of weed growing on rock. Everything else that comes along nests in the interstices between the narrow, soldierlike ranks of mussels. In order to render mussels fit for steaming, you have to tear away the weed, separate the colonies into individuals, toss out the ones too small to bother opening, and rinse the remainder in several buckets of water until the water stays clear.

And yet "when the tide is out, the table is set." The lowly mussel keeps himself impeccably clean inwardly; when properly steamed, fresh from his weedy bed, Mussels Maine shames Polipso and Marinara by comparison.

Pat added a dimension to Mussels Maine by bringing back some seaweed. She dumped a layer of that into the pail, then the mussels, then another layer, then enough steaming water to cover the bottom of the bucket. A fire under the pail kept the steam going and in less than thirty minutes well-steamed mussels were gaping wide, showing that they were done; we dipped them into melted butter and had them for dessert.

We watched the patterns of wind and rain dapple the surface of Winter Harbor in shifting soft metallic colors.

There are three main routes from the Penobscot to Mount Desert. The first is between mainland and Deer Isle—this is the lovely Eggemoggin Reach.

The second is between Deer Isle and Isle au Haut, and here you have a triple choice: Deer Island Thorofare, Merchants' Row, and Isle au Haut Thorofare. (See Map Eleven, page 150.)

The final choice is outside Isle au Haut which is far out of the way.

Of all these, Merchant's Row is the most interesting. It is dotted with little humped befirred granite globules of islands, green-gray jewels in a rich sea. You can have fair anchorage off either Saddleback or McGlathery, depending on wind. From either, you have a shot right across Blue Hill Bay to Mount Desert.

I figured my bearings carefully. The occasional deep bleat of horns from the direction of East Penobscot Bay warned that we'd have at least some fog outside. Additionally, nothing is as confusing as grouped islands of similar size.

We set off down our harbor somewhat after high

Map 11: Merchant's Row and Jericho Bay

1. SLIDE course from East Penobscot Bay and Vinalhaven.

2. Course to southern and eastern shore of Deer Isle.

3. Allen Cove, Deer Isle.

4. Stonington, Deer Island Thorofare.

5. Russ Island anchorage, Deer Island Thorofare.

6. Webb Cove anchorage. Off large new granite quarry.

7. Outer Southeast Harbor, Deer Isle.

8. Inner Southeast Harbor, Deer Isle.

9. Hawley Deep Hole, Southeast Harbor, Deer Isle.

10. Course to Isle au Haut and Isle au Haut Thorofare.

11. Pell Island Passage anchorage, Isle au Haut.

12. Burnt Island Thorofare, Isle au Haut.

13. York Ledges, Isle au Haut.

14. Round-McGlathery anchorage, Merchant's Row.

15. Saddleback Island mooring, Merchant's Row.

16. Course north through Jericho Bay to east end
of Eggemoggin Reach.

17. Course south through Jericho Bay to southern shore
of Swan's Island.

18. Burnt Coat Harbor, Swan's Island.

19. Buckle Harbor, off Casco Passage, Swan's Island.

20. Mackerel Cove, off Casco Passage, Swan's Island.

21. SLIDE course to Mount Desert and Blue Hill Bay
(see Map Twelve, page 160).

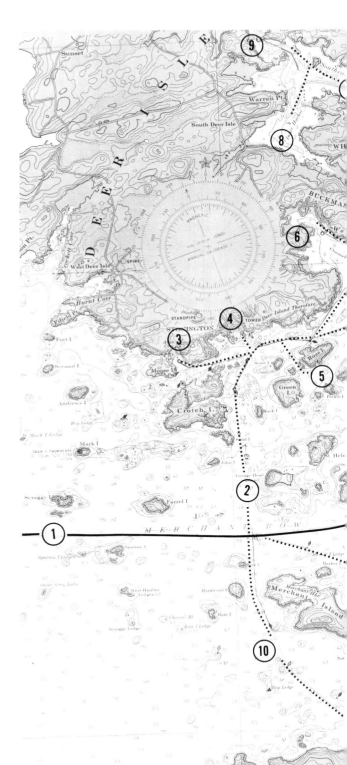

This is a planning aid; use only U.S. Geodetic charts for navigation.

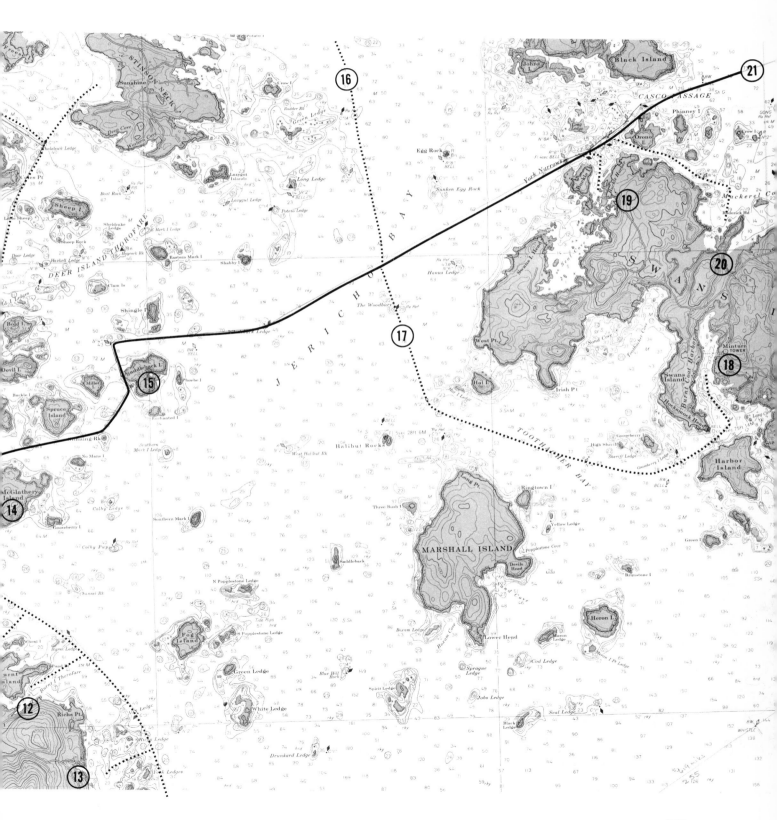

slack. The inlet had a vastly different look from when we had come in at low. Winter Harbor now appeared to be clear of rocks, as if you could go straight out the mouth. In fact, skirting the obvious rock groups you could see, you very probably could.

We left lots of things for our next visit to Winter Harbor: the walk to the swimming pond on the road which passes the head of Vinal Cove; a climb up Starboard Rock; a run of the dinghy under the bridge on Calderwood Neck (second indentation west of Starboard Rock) to Mill Basin and out into Fox Island Thorofare (what a route that would be if it were cruisable at low tide in a larger craft!). This is Maine's lure —the imagined surprises around the corners you didn't have time to turn.

East Penobscot Bay looked like the back of a great silver fox. Cool, chill gray-and-white colors shifted seaward on the surface and long lines of wavering fog banks topped the surface. Sea mist and gray overhead were rifted with swaths of darker stuff. We moved in a changing world and held course 100 for Buoy 2BC on the approach to Merchant's. In fact, I eventually began to wonder where in thunder Whistle Buoy 2BC was. It was supposed to be three miles away from our exit at Winter Harbor, and my estimated time of arrival was up. I swung *Puff* about in a circle, glaring angrily at the compass; I did not want to head into possible fog without a good solid idea of where I went in.

Buoy 2BC was there, all right, as Pat pointed out; in the haze, I had taken it to be an indistinct little lobster pot buoy. (Distortion of size and perspective is common in this kind of weather.) The whistle was tilted crazily to one side, which was one reason I interpreted "pot buoy." We went on past it at reduced speed for the gray-green island peaks of Merchant's Row ahead all looming up like volcanic tops above the cool wraiths of the smoke curtain.

Whistle 2BC is also where you'd take off for Stonington if you needed to supply your yacht at this point; in that case you would probably overnight in Webb Cove. (Further on in this chapter we visit both.)

South of us now was the bulk of Isle au Haut, which was discovered by Champlain and named by him for its high, 500-foot peak. I have climbed the trail to the top for a look at the territory around and it gives a splendid view of the Penobscot. The walk itself is a good change from being at sea when leg muscles have been cramped by too many days of no walking about. Isle au Haut has a grocery, and an old church; altogether, the island is simple and charming. Its people are also "old stock" and handy. Back in the middle of the last century a group of islanders built themselves a bark and with it sailed around Cape Horn to join the California Gold Rush.

Isle au Haut Thorofare is filling in. The eastern end at the beautiful passage between Isle au Haut and Kimball's Island is now down to about six feet.

On this cruise, as we tailed away from the whistle, I noted a certain serration of the silhouette of Sparrow Ledge just south of the course; a series of protuberances larger than those which would be caused by gulls or cormorants caught my eye. It was a group of harbor seals. Naturally the camera with the telescopic lens was unloaded so I had Pat do some lazy circles while I went below, hunted up some Tri-X, loaded, took a reading with the meter, and then pointed my lens. Seals are no one's fools; they had already noted our interest and had started sliding in the direction of the water. (Had we gunned by at full speed, they would have merely turned their heads.) As I took pictures, some of them fanned out in front, swimming toward the boat in the form of a circle centered on the ledge. Left on the ledge were three little ones, unstirring, and one adult. It seemed as though here was a natural maneuver to draw attention from the babies.

The seals swam for the boat until about twenty yards off, ducking up to stare unblinking and ducking down again. Only when almost under the bow did they disappear ensemble and stay down. We went off. Looking back, I could see several seals humping their way back up to the offspring, content with their strategy.

Merchant's Row showed us shifting scenes. In some perspectives, the group was a gathering of symmetrical crowned isles in an Aegean setting; in views taking in more of the bare islets, the islands looked definitely Aleutian against the sleek silver sky. Round Island was a boy's crayon of an island, rising to a conical cap with rod-straight firs forming the top. As we came in on Saddleback, we passed Enchanted, which is a bit like castle and keep, with its neat little "drawbridge" of sand. (Come sunny weather tomorrow, we'd be lying on the sand in the morning.) Luckily, the available mooring south of Saddleback was unused: a white topped log with heavy line on it. The small cottage on the point east of the bay showed us there was no one about so we tied to. A mooring seemed like a very fine thing to have: rain was coming in again, and the bottom here was very likely rocky. We didn't have to search for a spot that would hold the flukes of the Danforth anchor. The radio forecast light northeast winds, so we were presumably on the right anchorage in the islands. Saddleback shelters from the north and east (as McGlathery does from the south and west).

We secured our cockpit covering; the drops slid down the transparent side curtains and pattered a homily on top. Pat, resigned to the fact of cans, opened and prepared several whose contents neatly complemented each other while I sat down to some reading. My theory on cruise reading is to have paperbacks that you would never read in a mood of sober improvement. Tolkien's *The Hobbit* filled the bill exactly.

The warmth dropped with the sun and I broke out my *pièces de résistance* to cold: insulated long under-

wear, gear which makes any climate feel hot and dry. Last time I had had them on, I remembered, was on a chair lift at Stowe, Vermont, with the temperature six below at the summit and a twenty-mile wind blowing. At that point they meant survival; at this, they merely meant extreme comfort.

*Tuesday, August 23.* We awakened to the sound of rain sluicing against the cockpit roof and side curtains. I got up to make sure our mooring hadn't moved, because we were in a good twenty- to twenty-five-knot blow. By the compass it was southwest. We were on the wrong island.

One of the pleasures of bad weather is staying "slug-a-bed." There is no incentive to make tracks in this kind of weather, especially with a sea making up. I finally roused spontaneously at the laggard hour of nine thirty. The sea was starting to roll *Puff* more than a bit as we lay off the slick wet shelf of Saddleback's south shore.

If there is one thing that will move me, it is the rolling of an outboard hull at anchor. This roll has nothing in common with the gentle and rhythmic cradling motions of a well-ballasted sailing vessel at anchor in a humped sea; it is more akin to the motions of a tethered horse seeing a disliked rider approaching.

I proposed breakfast and then a quick run to the anchorage between Round Island and McGlathery where we could be in the calm and could also nip ashore to pick up a few mussels and clams. We would also be a couple of miles nearer Stonington, where we'd planned to stop for supplies.

By the time we'd upped the anchor there was a stiff breeze outside. The rollers were cresting slightly, showing white breaks in the shades of lead, gray, and dark green. The wet and windy scene had its own kind of beauty; setting it off was loud breaking of the sea on the rock shores as we angled by. I thought now of the

*A freshwater stream enters*
*into a brine pool formed in one of*
*Winter Harbor's old granite workings*

many, many ships gone down on windward shores in Maine before the days of engine on this coast. One of our islands to starboard was called Wreck Island and it had indubitably earned its name.

In truth, if our engines had died then and there, we would have been in about the same pickle as the ancient mariners. This is why I like to build up a few layers of safety against the occurrence of such last-ditch situations. It is why I prefer two forty-horse engines to one eighty, although the eighty might be more efficient: it is highly unlikely that two engines will go bad at once.

I was carrying two Danforth anchors, each with two hundred feet of the best nylon line I could lay my hands on. (They were beautifully made by the Samson Cordage Company of Boston.) The chances of catching one or both Danforths pretty solidly in a dragging situation would be excellent; the elasticity of the nylon is a property that tends to keep the flukes of the Danforths from being broken out of good holding ground. Third, I had the dinghy with both motor and oars; fourth, of course, vest life jackets (none of your floating cushions).

So much for gloomy if valuable thoughts. We caught a lobster boat riding easily in the sea; the lobster fisherman stood nonchalantly at the helm, running over to a winch and winding the pots in as if this were the flattest, hottest day in the summer. His hull scudded off westward and we rode after, nosing down the lee side of the swells with engines speeding joyfully as we slid. It was thirty minutes' work to the very welcome calm of the harbor off Round and McGlathery which was perfectly sheltered from south winds. And the rain came in harder.

Nonetheless we dauntlessly went forth musseling, doubly armored in insulated underwear and foul weather gear. The shore of Round was alight with the purple sheen of mussel shell, set below and between the yellow of the seaweed and the subtle grays and browns of the granite ledge. It was too cold to bother about clam digging, so we simply snatched mussels like a couple of blueberry pickers, stopping at each patch to separate the live ones from the small cemeteries of empty mussel shell with which they seem to surround themselves.

Back on board, we steamed the mussels between layers of seaweed (almost no water needed since the seaweed gives up water under heat). Then we tidied up and belted our way over a short course to Stonington. Even I was beginning to admit to the attraction of fresh green salad, and we needed the usual water-oil-gas-ice quartet. We came in at Stonington to see most of her lobster fleet riding at anchor, some with their steadying sails still up, pointed nose down the channel east, head into the blow. The lobster boats were immaculate, and the hillful of Victorian buildings situated overlooking the main street and facing the harbor were houses that once obviously were built very expensively and to smart taste.

Deer Island, the second largest on Maine's coast (twenty-seven square miles) is a very special place in the American yachtsman's world. Deer Islanders crewed on some of the outstanding *America's* Cup defenders in the days when the Cup was raced in the huge J-boats, hulls more than twice the size of the present twelve-meter contestants. Not only was the greatest J-boat of all—*Ranger*—built in Bath but the great crews, those veritable hordes of faceless yet highly skilled men who trimmed the sheets and moved from side to side to act as human ballast—bent low so as to reduce wind resistance—these were Deer Islanders. Every man Jack of them had grown up on sailing craft.

In the early days, hundreds of sailcraft were built, manned, and run by the Deer Islanders in the normal course of a few years' business. The number of Deer Island's fleet once ran "as many as three hundred sail."

Well, they are gone. College boys man the *America*'s Cup defenders these days.

Deer Island still builds ships—trawlers. Her sailors are now mostly employed in lobster fishing, because her other fishing is gone. Of the old industries there remains only the granite. Just off Stonington, as we had come in, we had passed Crotch Island. Her high derricks jutted from invisible quarries on the island. Here it was that the granite for President Kennedy's memorial was being quarried. It's still the best granite in the country.

We tied to Stonington's Atlantic gas dock; as far as we could see, this was the only float among the piers at the port. We were next door to the Atlantic Hardware pier where the Crosier family sells lobster and clams in good weather. The Crosiers also sell ice from their home up the side of the hill in town. The wharfman at the gas float said that when it came to delivering ice to dockside, the Crosiers were "independent as a hog on ice." But the Crosier truck was at the pier and the nice young fellow driving said he'd take us to the house to get a block. He did. In the shed of the Crosiers' big New England farmhouse stood a feast of clams and lobster in baskets. The fact that we'd just devoured a more than sufficient intake of mussels saved us a lot of money right then.

The driver also offered to ride us to the state liquor store which lies at the western end of the main street; he helped even more by stopping at Bartlett's grocery where Pat spent her way into debt. I can recommend this town for supplies (the Atlantic Hardware store has good marine hardware to complete the picture). The only cavil, besides the fact that you might have a long walk for ice, is that the town water is notoriously heavy on chlorine and has a "tank taste." But it is perfectly drinkable.

We left Stonington with the idea of going to Webb Cove, one of the few well-protected harbors around, but we had a late start and after missing a buoy in the darkening waters and having an intimate look by flashlight at the number of reefs close to our intended course, we settled for the anchorage in an open cove just north of Russ Island, off Stonington. I knew—just knew—this would be a good deal rollier than the nice sheltered waters of Webb, but it could not be helped. After a good deal of hacking about, I had set the anchor well and tested it by backing the engines. I felt the tremors on the anchor line stop; this meant that the anchor had stopped dragging and that the flukes had sunk in. We were about halfway between the black can off Russ and the island itself; this gave me enough room to let out a hundred feet of line in what is about twenty feet of water at high tide.

A good deal more than wind protection goes into a good anchorage. The bottom should be fairly soft. A perfectly protected harbor with a smooth rock-ledge bottom would be useless, because even a very heavy mushroom anchor would tend to slide over this, and the tide would take you. Fortunately, there is usually a good covering of growth on rock bottoms and at least some clay or mud. In preference, one picks places that are marked "sft" (soft) or "stk" (sticky) on a chart in preference to "rky" (rocky). Even then, in "rky" places, your Danforth may quite readily catch in crevices or come to rest wedged in a pile of good-sized "rks."

Anyway, our anchor was down good and solid. The rollers from the southeaster were still running, hard. The radio announced west winds and blue sky for sure in the morning. (I never go to bed without listening to the weather. I remember the yachtsmen who missed the all-too-short warning of Hurricane Carol back in the 1950s and who also lost their yachts.)

There are so-called harbors of refuge, harbors where you can laugh even at a hurricane and, if a hurricane starts coming, I want to be on one of those harbors. In this part of the country the best would probably be

*Stonington: lobster fisherman's world*

Blue Hill. You have sufficient warnings of hurricane these days—what with weather satellites and all—to get out of the way.

The Heat Pal warmed the cabin to a nice temperature, and I don't remember feeling the slightest rocking motion after my head touched down.

*Wednesday, August 24.* My first thought on being rolled out of a sound slumber by the wake of a passing lobster boat—at the usual fisherman punching-in time—was that the wind had augmented. But everything was fine. I tumbled back into bed, only barely noting that the clouds were starting to lift and lighten. An hour later, I really got up.

I decided to pursue my thought that there was nice quiet water in Webb Cove. And so there was. We rounded the corner into the cove and proceeded to skirt the huge fish weir, going north of it, and so into the inner harbor. A huge new granite quarry had been cut on the north shore. The spiderweb guy wires balanced the two huge block-lifting derricks and a great storage shed had been constructed up the shore. The face of the quarry was blocked out by the cutting. This is probably the only place on the Maine coast where you can look right into the heart of a working granite quarry from on deck.

We had no sooner anchored than a dynamite blast from the quarry signaled that operations had commenced. From time to time, great truckloads of granite were dumped down the side of the road toward the water a hundred feet away. But the noise was not bad. It was merely an occasional dull roar. We finished breakfast as a couple in a canoe came paddling out from the edge of the inner bay. They came up with practiced strokes—a man and a woman who had done much paddling together. They told us that we were in a spot that went dry at low. We thanked them and they paddled off toward the sea. I wondered if this was a

routine that they followed ritualistically through the summer: out canoeing before the tide runs out and back home again when the bay filled up full. I wondered out loud why anyone would buy a summer place on a bay that was dry twice in twenty-four hours. Pat said that land was probably cheaper.

Now welcome fingers of west wind crept across the surface of the bay and seemed to push open the dreary cover that lidded the sky. A veritable silver spot appeared in the east, shedding light, spendthrift. It was the first sun we'd seen in two days. The forces of light gathered strength and clefts of blue broke here and there, and the silver sun yellowed and turned to bright bullion, an alchemy that gladdened.

A flock of gulls ashore were circling a piece of some gull goody on a rock. A white gull held the fort and the others circled with piercing piteous sounds while the king of the rock ate his fill. Then a young gull appeared, swooped in, and preempted the spot: the old king abdicated hastily. It was as if this fight had already been decided and, the outcome being known, it behooved the older gull not to uselessly repeat it.

The bottom was coming into view, washing up out of the water as the tide ran; land was slowly closing in on *Puff* from all sides. Pat took the helm and got us on the outside of the little island in the bay. Here *Puff* would stay wet. As the sun came out, it warmed deliciously. Wet and damp clothing laid out in the cockpit began to evaporate dew and show nap and weave instead of a soggy surface.

I remember looking ashore before we left. A young man was wading along the strand in fishing boots, neither clamming nor working, but just walking along, going nowhere in particular, with a warm midmorning sun lighting up every drop that he jetted around his boots. The scene had all the innocence of a lost age.

We motored out along the quarry and it was not without a certain twinge that I left the rest of Deer Isle untouched on this cruise. What sights we had missed! There was one exploration that I longed to try. Just north of us, Southeast Harbor on Deer Isle leads to Long Cove where lies Hawleys Deep Hole, a place that is supposed to be both beautiful and dangerous. I'd love to get there and push around in the dinghy. On the far side of Deer Isle lies Sylvester Cove, another of the beauty inlets of the coast and of course there are a number of harbors in Eggemoggin Reach worth visiting. But we didn't because we couldn't, without racing about too much, do more than we had.

Our course was to Mount Desert: we'd stayed our week in the Penobscot. And the high road to Mount Desert was as the cover of a slick yachting magazine. The whole sea to the far, dim outline of the mountains of Mount Desert was one brilliant and sparkling field of burning cobalt broken by white flags of cresting chop. Here and there a tossing mane hung over a ledge.

We came zooming over the pitch and roll of Jericho Bay out of our small island world south of Deer Isle. We were aiming for York Narrows, the southern route through Casco Passage. It is better marked and more interesting than the northern route; the alternate nuns and cans led us handily (Map Twelve, page 160).

South of Casco Passage was Swans Island, a big (sixth largest in Maine, ten square miles) island with an eminently explorable coastline. It has at least three good harbors, including the long lovely Burnt Coat Harbor on the south shore. The island is named for a very romantic and strange gentleman, Colonel James Swan of Boston. Swan was one of the Sons of Liberty who dumped tea into Boston Harbor; further, he was wounded at Bunker Hill, was given a fortune by an old Scotsman who admired him. With that, he made lots more money and built himself a beautiful home at West and Tremont Streets in Boston. He also bought and built up Swan's Island in Maine, thinking to turn it into a productive country estate. But he was seldom

there, being now engaged in supplying the French Army. Then suddenly he was arrested in Paris for a debt he swore he didn't owe. Although he could have paid it, rather than pay a "false debt," he spent twenty-two years in jail. He was freed after a change of regimes in France and went to see his old friend Lafayette, once more. And then, since his wife had died and he was now getting on, he decided to return to jail where all his remaining friends were.

It all reads like the purplish prose of a feverish author, but it is as actual as the island that now bears Swan's name.

We were drawing a straight line north of Swan's to Mount Desert: we gunned for Bass Head Light on a course of 93 Magnetic, a course only three degrees off the 100 percent Down East course of 90 Magnetic.

A powerboat, particularly one with twin screws, has running habits in common with a cruising sail yacht. If you substitute the trim of the power hull for the trim of an auxiliary's sail, and the balance of the throttles for the balance of the sailing helm, you will see that pushing a powerboat around is not just a function of advancing the throttles with a twitch of the biceps. In the first place, the hull has to sit level. It's no good careening across the waters at a photogenic heel because that is making one engine work harder than the other. Secondly, just as a lee or a weather helm deadens a sailing yacht's best qualities, so with twin screws. There is a balance where the twin props will sing and go that extra 10 percent; to an attuned sensitivity, this is the difference between slogging and sprinting. I had been experimenting with various differentials of gas weight between the two cockpit tanks and had played with the length of the dinghy line (dinghy drag is a decided factor in a light rig). Today I seemed to have hit it because *Puff* really went. She was going 16 and 17 mph —superlative when you figure the weather, her gross and cargo.

Map 12: *Jericho Bay, Blue Hill Bay, and Mount Desert*

1. SLIDE course through Merchant's Row.

2. Pell Island Passage anchorage, Isle au Haut.

3. Burnt Coat Thorofare, Isle au Haut.

4. York Ledges anchorage, Isle au Haut.

5. Course into Southeast Harbor, Deer Isle.

6. Sunshine anchorage, Deer Isle.

7. Center Harbor, Brooklin, eastern mouth of Eggemoggin Reach.

8. Course to western mouth of Eggemoggin Reach.

9. Benjamin River harbor, Eggemoggin Reach.

10. Course to northern shores of Mount Desert and Mount Desert Narrows.

11. Course north in Blue Hill Bay to the upper bay and the harbor of Blue Hill town.

12. Buckle Harbor, Casco Passage, Swan's Island.

13. Mackerel Cove, Casco Passage, Swan's Island.

14. Burnt Coat Harbor, Swan's Island.

15. Goose Cove, western shores of Mount Desert Island.

16. Seal Cove, Mount Desert Island.

17. Bass Harbor, Mount Desert Island.

18. Gott Islands anchorage.

19. Western Way, passage to inner harbors of Mount Desert.

20. Cranberry Harbor, Islesboro.

21. Manset, Southwest Harbor, Mount Desert Island. Home of the Hinckley yard.

22. Southwest Harbor town, Southwest Harbor, Mount Desert.

23. Somes Sound entrance, beginning of six-mile fjord into the heart of Mount Desert Island.

24. Northeast Harbor, Mount Desert.

25. Seal Harbor, Eastern Way, Mount Desert.

26. Course up the eastern shore of Mount Desert past Bar Harbor.

27. SLIDE course across Frenchman's Bay to the Schoodic Peninsula.

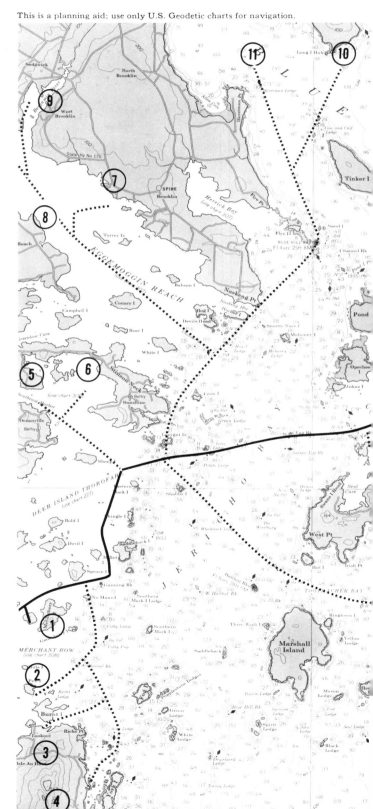

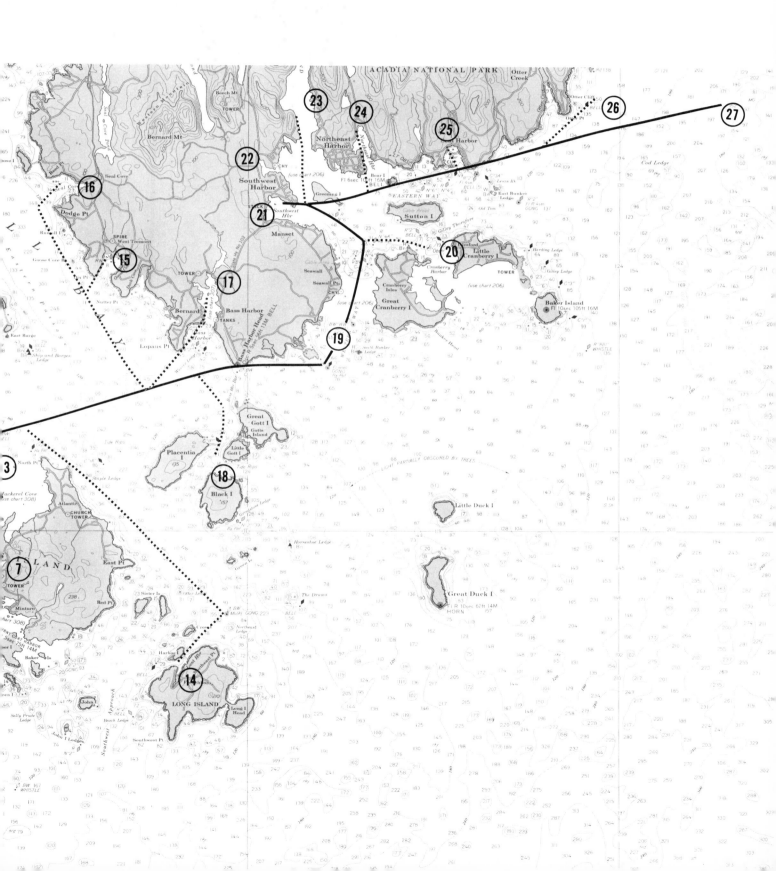

*Puff* came on like Gangbusters through Casco Passage and then we were on the wide open of Blue Hill Bay; the undulant exciting shapes of the heights of Mount Desert began to define themselves more clearly on the skyline.

This is the point at which, had we planned a side trip to Frenchboro in Lunts Harbor on Long Island, we'd have doglegged south around the top of Swans Island. However, since we were counting on picking up Lunts Harbor coming back, we would bypass it now.

We were now well into Blue Hill Bay, which is a cruising ground in itself going far into the north; once more grounds we'd have to forgo. Finally, we were free of all the islands and looking clearly at the Mount Desert hills. Mount Desert is the most famous single name on the coast of Maine. Not only does this island contain Bar Harbor, the locus of the earliest "rich man's beach" on the coast, but it is a big island, 16 miles long and 12 miles wide, 107 square miles in all. This makes it the country's second biggest Atlantic coast island (the largest is Long Island, N.Y.) Just slightly more massive than Martha's Vineyard, Mount Desert is also set with the country's highest East Coast headland, Mount Cadillac, 1,532 feet above sea level. This is the highest point on land north of Rio de Janeiro.

Mount Desert contains both subarctic and temperate zone characteristics and species belonging to both zones, fauna and flora. It is a place for fishermen, naturalists, nature lovers, and sailors.

From a sailing point of view, Mount Desert's great feature is the space in the center of the island where the salt water flows in to form three large harbors: Northeast, Southwest, and Somes. The latter is a straight, broad, enclosed, seven-mile stretch; it has been called "the only true fjord on the Atlantic Coast" because of its high, mountainous western shore.

During the Revolution the island of Mount Desert ruled itself by town meeting and probably never saw a

*Mattie and* Mercantile *racing
in to Somes Sound, Mt. Desert*

federal or Massachusetts officer (Maine was part of Massachusetts then) from one decade to the next. Some of the independence must have stuck: when my father was on the Maine liquor commission, there were certain unspecified illegalities carried on by the natives which were long undetectable. Every time a liquor inspector crossed the bridge, the signal went out to the whole "tight little island" and nary a drop was to be found. The commission solved the problem by sneaking inspectors across the bridge under canvas in the back of an open truck. That worked well once, anyway.

We now closed in rapidly on Western Way, sliding up to the elegant lighthouse at Bass Harbor on the near corner of the island and, proceeding, we turned and headed sharp north where Great Cranberry Island forms, with Mount Desert, the aforesaid Western Way, the nearest approach to the island's interior harbors.

We had arrived at a wonderful moment. In the Western Way ahead of us were the two huge Maine lumber schooners now converted to cruise ships, *Mattie* and *Mercantile*. What better way to come into Maine's most yachty ports than with these two on a fabulous August noon? They were hard on the wind across the stretch from Great Cranberry to Greening Island; *Mercantile* had the lead. This was how schooner captains of old raced each other into port in their day with a round of rum at stake and much bragging and sly digging afterwards on the part of the winners and imperturbable rationalizations on the part of the losers.

It might have been the Maine of a hundred years ago: I couldn't even register the small motor yachts and fiber glass day sailers that came out to see the schooners in. My eyes were riveted on the long sloping lines of the two majestic hulls, on their raking foremasts and mains, on their canvas that dwarfed everything else.

We finally ran up beside them and followed as they went north of Greening and turned the corner into

Somes Sound; they followed the long funnel of water due north into the heart of the high rock of Mount Desert; surely one of the very rarest sights on the coast was the *Mercantile* and the *Mattie* in this body of water. As they raced ahead, *Mercantile* seemed a bit more close-winded than *Mattie* (even though the rig and proportions of the latter are far more rakish and photogenic). *Mercantile* ran straight down the middle while *Mattie* had to take a couple of tacks. I couldn't see the reason for the difference. The only obvious thing was that *Mercantile* had a ramrod-straight stalwart at the wheel while *Mattie* was sailed by an old fellow, bent to his task, peering over the spokes. Maybe the older man was not about to strap her down tight and make her point up; maybe he just didn't care and was content to let her run a bit off the wind and to tack about.

We finally stopped our chase. I turned *Puff* into Valley Cove, the most spectacular anchorage in Somes. Here, the high heads of Flying Mountain, Valley Peak, St. Sauveur and Acadia hung over the water in spectacular walls, amply protecting us by their six hundred vertical feet. It was so calm here, I simply shut the engines down and we drifted about enjoying the duel of the giants from afar. Pat made up a lunch while we drifted. *Mercantile* and *Mattie* came about and then came reaching back past us on their way out with the bow waves licking their hull planks as the schooners headed for their next harbor, still racing.

The strip of field off a sand beach at the foot of Flying Mountain here is one of history's favorite spots. It was here that the first real face-to-face of the French and English in this new continent took place. In 1613 a group of Jesuits settled on the shore, having come this way via the French settlement on the St. Croix to the east. Mount Desert thus became the first mission in the New World on the Atlantic Coast. Unhappily for the Jesuits, they had only time to convert a few Indians

before the arrival of the "Admiral of Virginia" (and "Virginia" at that time included Maine, according to the charter of the Virginia Company). Samuel Argall, coming on the scene in his sailing ship, attacked the Jesuit camp and simply wiped the missionaries out. Clean slate. England and France were not yet at war so this was a considerable provocation and there was an exchange of acid notes across the English Channel on the matter.

Also, on this same strip of land, a thousand years ago, so it is supposed, the first historic confrontation between the Old World and the New took place. Vikings out of Leif Erikson's original encampment in North America, "Vinland Camp," fought it out with a tribe of Indians or, as the Vikings called them, "Skraelings" ("Screamers").

The supposition is based on the saga's description of an expedition by Leif Erikson's brother Thorvald to a "fjord" north of Vinland. Thorvald landed and found the land "fair." He said he'd make his camp here. The Vikings, with their usual Nordic straightforwardness, killed off some eight Indians they found on the strand. One Indian escaped. The next morning the Viking ship was attacked by canoeloads of furious Indians, according to the sagas. One Indian arrow wounded Thorvald fatally. After the Indians had been repulsed the crew buried Thorvald on the land he'd liked so much. If Vinland, as some claim, was south of Mount Desert, very likely Thorvald's bones and rusted armor still lie somewhere under Flying Mountain.

On the other hand, the new discovery of the seemingly authentic remains of a Viking camp in Newfoundland may place the site of "Vinland" north of Mount Desert; if so, then we may look for Thorvald elsewhere.

Much, much later Mount Desert was the Newport of its time. The places from that era still standing along the shore are nothing if not spectacular: rustic, shaded,

Edwardian or Victorian: there was less accent on architectural grandeur than with the later castles of Newport but more accent here on displaying the land. Typically, a mansion at Mount Desert stands on a five- or six-acre swath of cleared land—green grass and gold hay—bounded by the backdrop of virgin fir and spruce. It is ostentation in a quiet way, a way that you have to be bred to; you could not buy it even if you had the money.

But now we had yacht business to attend to so—over to Southwest Harbor. The little settlement, Manset, on the southern shore of Southwest is the home of Hinckley, the most famous yacht builder in Maine. And the Hinckley yard is the friend of all coastwise yachtsmen and the baby sitter for their troubles; it is also the showplace of coastwise yachting in the state.

One thing that makes Hinckley such a show is that Hinckley is building a spanking new series of fiber glass sailing auxiliaries; if you can afford one you have the *outre*, the apogee of sailing auxiliaries. Hinckleys run from thirty to forty-eight feet and cost approximately a thousand dollars a foot without sails or instruments. The Hinckley forty-foot center boarder is the sweetest design I've seen in an age. It has a great deal of deck space on each side of the cabin; the foredeck is lawn-size. The one thing that I miss on most auxiliaries is lying-down space somewhere outside the cockpit.

I spent an hour wandering about on the Hinckley floats—they have three going out from the wharf in tandem—looking first at one and then the other. I began to calculate how many copies of this book I would have to sell in order to buy that forty-footer. I stopped at the point where the book had passed the combined sales of *Gone with the Wind* and the Revised Standard Bible. (Reader, do not believe that the sale of a few thousand sets an author up for life, please.)

The number of things that have to be done in such a locale as Hinckley's are innumerable. Shoptalking, chart-scanning, and one-upping with the cruising clan (I hate to gossip but it's the only way to keep up), fueling, icing (cake and cubes), groceries—there's one at Manset (in fact, here is a microcosm of a town built especially for yachtsmen), telephoning ("I've had a little trouble, boss, and I'll have to extend to Labor Day"), arrival-watching, rig-buying ("I'll take that brass snap and charge it"). In sum, we stayed long. Since it was not a busy time (on weekends float space is a fight), we cooked dinner tied to the float.

Sitting there on *Puff*, we watched the tide carrying a river of purple shifting wavelets out to sea. The sky turned fiery pink as the already-set sun touched the waves with promise of fair weather tomorrow.

I was sweet-scented, having availed myself of Hinckley's free luxury, a hot shower. I helped Pat turn the fried chicken over the charcoal grill. At this juncture, I was reminded of a passage from a book on dry-land cruising (hiking) *The Hard Way to Haparanda* done by a very literate Englishman. After extolling the virtues of hiking, the author goes on to say that the very *best* thing about it all is that wonderful feeling when you stop.

We spent the night at a proffered mooring off Hinckley's. Since the sea tends to roll here and the wake of arrivals is a fairly constant phenomenon—twenty-four hours a day—I could reflect that my intention of spending the night in the sheltered waters off Islesford in the Cranberry Isles outside Southwest was just another one of the stones with which the road to perdition is traditionally paved.

Chance, *a sturdy old Friendship sloop,*
*in Southwest Harbor, Mt. Desert*

THURSDAY, AUGUST 25. This morning was spent in the happy occupation: doing the Grand Tour of the cliffs on the foreside of Mount Desert in the Eastern Way. To begin our tour, we motored out of Southwest, speeded on past Northeast, then puttered along Bracy's Cove (next east from Northeast), then past Seal Cove (home of the Rockefellers), and finally reached the intriguing cliffs around Hunter's Beach and Otter Cove.

Here we also sailed with a venerable old Friendship sloop, *Chance,* built by Wilbur Morse in 1916. *Chance* was on a family outing. With her huge gaff and double head rig, she seemed as sturdy and delightfully old-fashioned to us as she must have to the family now aboard and to all the families that had owned *Chance* in fifty years.

We nosed slowly about taking pictures of reefs where the surge was tossing spectacular white plumes straight up the ledge formations under the high skyward bight of Cadillac Mountain shouldering up past slightly less elevated behemoths on both sides; the mountains formed a massive arched skyline of pink and salmon and moss gray-green.

Now we steered back down the Eastern Way, to Northeast and anchored off the western shore for lunch, bobbing in a mild chop. Northeast is a small and very swanky harbor. This must suit the owners of the large, marvelous, dormered, peaked, and verandaed, three-story Victorian era vacation homes set on the cliffs on both sides of the neat little harbor. After our lunch we went into the harbor marina. Clifton's has a phone and ice, gas and oil and a yachtsman's lounge, some yachting supplies—in all, a very nice place to find in such a small and noncommercial harbor.

A man with white hair was zipping around the harbor in a purple-hulled, high-horsepower, purple-upholstered runabout, evidently as passionate about his craft as its colors indicated; he reveled in putting on little bursts of speed to start up a bantam rooster tail from time to time. A younger outboarder skimmed by in a junior racing rig: an Evinrude six mounted high on a "shingle" hull. The kid had a crash helmet and all. Then, as we waited for our tanks to fill, we saw a small sailing catamaran breezing by—a Pacific Cat. It had the upright mast and the fast acceleration that make these craft a fascination. If they would only build a dry one.

We were parked across the float from a very big sixty-footer, probably with twin PT engines under the deck and obviously with radar on the mast. I consoled myself with the thought that there was no place she could go we couldn't go. Contrarywise, there were lots of places we could go she couldn't. If I had the $85,000 she probably cost, I'd be tempted to bank eighty and spend five on *Puff TMD.* (This was her cost as she stood outfitted.)

The rotund, satisfied owner of this U.S.S. Big was standing on the float, deep in conversation with the crew sitting on an auxiliary alongside. I heard the pretty wife on the auxiliary say, in rising inflections, "And that's you over there?" pointing to his yacht. It certainly was.

And this is me, over here, lady. If you think that any man who can go to sea in an outboard hull isn't tough as nails (wooden hulls and iron men), you're wrong. And that's my yacht club flag there on the mast: a rattlesnake on a field of white.

Actually, I do carry a yacht club flag. I've never had to fly it to get service at a private yacht club on any coast but you never can tell. It is the flag of the Cobbosseecontee Yacht Club, one of the oldest clubs in the country; that's a fact. It was founded by gentlemen residing on the shores of said lake in 1870 and the flag has been carried all over the world by us Cobbossee yachtsmen at one time or another. The club currently has several hundred motoring members and thirty or so sailing members. Its Flying Tern fleet is the cham-

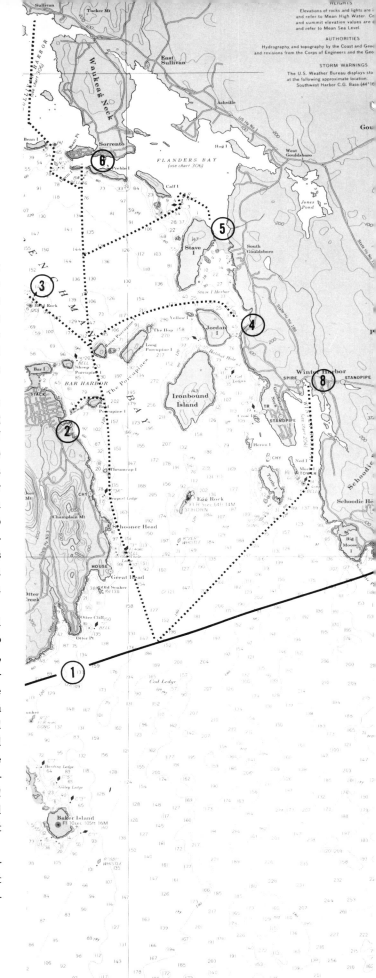

pion of the Flying Tern world. And, as long as I don't look it up in Lloyd's Register of Yachts, I can be relatively secure in the knowledge that Cobbosseecontee Yacht Club, by virtue of longevity alone, must perforce be classed as one of those "recognized yacht clubs" to which other clubs are bound to extend courtesy and recognition. Our membership is a good buy on that account alone because annual dues are one dollar.

We got out of Northeast after lunch just in time to catch the lovely *Victory Chimes* under full sail tacking toward Southwest. I was determined to have a shot of *Puff* alongside the venerable monster, so I hopped into the dinghy and let Pat drive *Puff* on a parallel course. (*Puff* looked like a little happy penguin splashing after a surfaced whale.) The big schooner came by me with impressive presence: she was doing a good ten to twelve, maybe better, in the fine southwest breeze, condescendingly heeling a bit, hardly rising in the swells but letting them surge by her flanks. It was really a grand sight, especially from my vantage point half a foot above the water, sitting in *X-ray*.

*Victory Chimes* has appeared in so many coastal shots of Maine (it's the only three-master going up here, so you know that it is she) that I have thought, why not go one better and have the Federal Government kick in enough to re-create one of the old Maine clipper ships, say the *Red Jacket?* Let that serve as an Outward Bound-type training ship for lads who could benefit. The ascent of any clipper ship shroud in a good breeze certainly ought to rank with spending three nights on a deserted island in terms of character-building. Think of the publicity that would be generated! And the jobs. One such ship on the Maine coast would bring several thousand cruising men up to see just that sight. Not to mention tourists.

After I got back aboard *Puff*, we split away from *Victory Chimes* and started collecting red nuns at a great rate, clipping down the Eastern Way toward French-

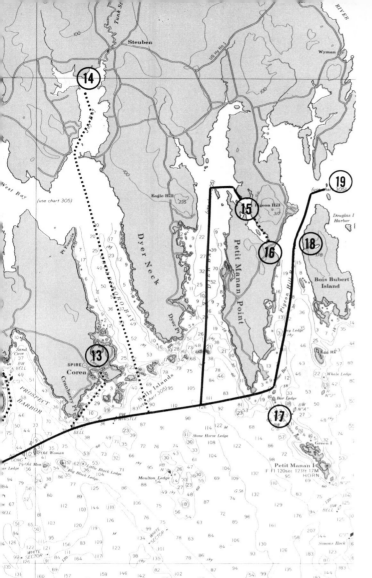

*Map 13: Mount Desert to Bois Bubert Island*

1. SLIDE course from Eastern Way, Mount Desert, across Frenchman's Bay to Schoodic.

2. Bar Harbor, Frenchman's Bay, eastern shore of Mount Desert.

3. Course to Mount Desert Narrows.

4. Stave Island anchorage, Schoodic Peninsula.

5. Flanders Bay anchorage, Schoodic Peninsula.

6. Sorrento Harbor at the head of Frenchman's Bay.

7. Sullivan Harbor.

8. Winter Harbor, Schoodic Peninsula, western shore.

9. Schoodic Point.

10. Bunker Harbor. Picturesque fishing village and sheltered mooring.

11. Birch Harbor, Schoodic Peninsula.

12. Prospect Harbor, Schoodic Peninsula.

13. Corea Harbor, Corea Town, Schoodic Peninsula. Fine fishing village.

14. Joy Bay anchorage at the head of Gouldsboro Bay between Dyer Neck and Schoodic Peninsula.

15. Carrying Place Cove at the head of Dyer Bay between Dyer Neck and Petit Manan Point.

16. Pigeon Hill. A landmark at the head of dinghy run down Carrying Place Cove.

17. Petit Manan Point and Petit Manan Bar.

18. Big Head anchorage off Bois Bubert Island, opposite the town of Pigeon Hill on Pigeon Hill Bay.

19. SLIDE course to Narragaugus Bay, Cape Split, and Jonesport (see Map Fourteen, page 184).

This is a planning aid; use only U.S. Geodetic charts for navigation.

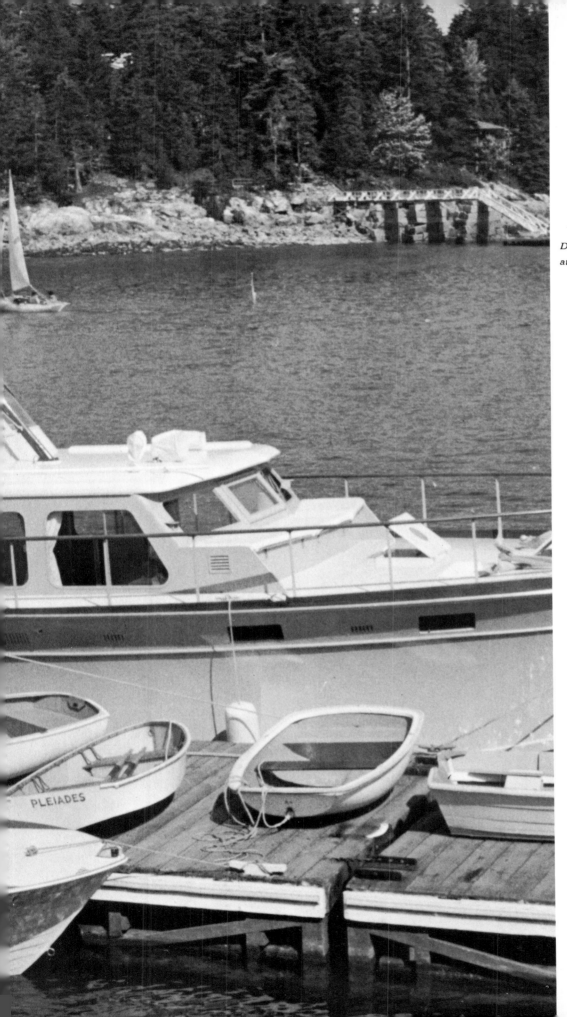

*Docked with a behemoth*
*at Northeast Harbor, Mt. Desert*

man's Bay, taking a 100 percent Down East course of 90 Magnetic. The eight-mile run to Schoodic Peninsula across the deep would bring us to the last section of Maine on our cruise: the Eastern Coast, a section which stretches clear up to Canada. We would go about halfway into this section before turning around.

The ocean's own blue hills of water were moving majestically in from the Atlantic over Frenchman's and we rolled over them. We met splendidly caparisoned yachts, knights of the sea in full regalia, running free toward Mount Desert and Casco Passage beyond to taste the joys we had so recently sampled.

Our SLIDE course gave us Bunker Harbor next, a good niche at the outer edge of Prospect Harbor just beyond Schoodic, reportedly the Williamsburg of lobster fishing villages; it has a cluster of small frame houses at the waterside and a small fleet of lobster boats at anchor in view of the homes. It is as if preserved intact from a generation ago. And besides, Bunker fits superbly with the SLIDE precept, being just off the shortest course (Map Thirteen, page 168).

We'd be skipping the delights of Upper Frenchman's Bay where lie Bar Harbor on the Mount Desert side and Sorrento on the mainland side; the latter has an unparalleled view of the sea and of Cadillac Mountain. We'd also be skipping the run under the bridge at Mount Desert Narrows, a run I mean to make in a shoal draft boat someday.

Across Frenchman's Bay, *Puff TMD* had a rollicking ride, going as well and as fast as she has ever done. We were aiming between Schoodic and Schoodic Island, bypassing the mouth of Winter Harbor, to the north, another pretty place. We left it behind this trip in order to have enough time to enjoy the marvelous waters off Jonesport.

Behind us were the grand green-and-blue, rose-and-pink pachyderm hills of Mount Desert. All of Frenchman's Bay lay to port and all the water of the Gulf of Maine to starboard. Full throttle: *X-ray* was hopping in our wake like a mad transparent bunny, weaving frantic patterns in the backlit waters. Off the bow, fast materializing, was the faint pink and dun projection of Schoodic. This peninsula is a ragged, much-worn strip of rock, bruised and broken with the effort of resisting the combers that constantly lunge at her over the bar and strike with photogenic explosions; as we came closer it was as if depth charges were being set off around her base, flinging geysers of white high into the air.

To starboard the great white shaft of Schoodic Light brooded over Schoodic Island. As we drew even with the light, I got out in *X-ray* to shoot a few frames of our boat passing the peninsula. The surge, impelled by the bar below, swung the little dinghy up and down; the effect was of a huge watery teeter-totter which had me shifting my weight side to side to keep me dry; even the little bit of very cold sea which slopped over the sides from time to time was more than enough to remind my toes of what total immersion off here would be like. I was more than glad to climb back onto *Puff* when Pat had circled back.

And then we rounded Schoodic; the surge subsided somewhat and we bore in on Bunker Harbor.

As it was reputed, so it was: we found that the small-scale chart, 305, scarcely did Bunker justice. (Advice: stick to the south shore; there is plenty of water around the high rock at the southern entrance to the outer harbor. You will thus avoid trouble with the ledge marked on the chart toward the middle of the entrance.) There was a round, somewhat sheltered outer harbor with a stone beach, and deep water right to the entrance of the inner harbor; inside this, the ten or twelve boats of the lobster fishing fleet lay pointed in a parallel direction; ashore were the small, well-kept-up fishermen's homes; there were no incongruous large Victorian structures as at Stonington. It was a perfect

Maine fishing harbor.

It was now high tide; we got a ten-foot sounding on the Raytheon when we tried it south of the fleet anchorage; with the ten-foot tide here, this didn't seem quite enough. I was trying to figure out a safe place where we could swing without tangling with the fleet when a lobster fisherman came rowing out to tell us we were sitting over a ledge. "Wouldn't lie here," he said, "you might ground out." He told us to pick up an empty mooring on the other side of the fleet. We thanked him.

We asked if there were any lobster to be bought. He said that there was a lobster pound at the head of the harbor but that the catch was marked for a firm in Rockland; the only way was to get one off a fisherman. The fishermen were now all ashore; he halloed to a fisherman who was sitting on a porch to ask if there were any lobster for sale. The man ashore halloed back, "No, I haven't any." And then *he* hailed the man next door who said he'd sold his. At the very least, we began to feel welcome.

After we moored, I took *X-ray* into the pound and talked to the pound master who said he'd asked one of the men who was just going out to pull traps in the outer harbor to come by our boat. I thanked him and sat down as is polite. You don't break off hurriedly in Maine.

I found out that this place has a regular small lake beyond it which forms the "pound"; this, rather than the well of the wood lobster float (a "lobster car") is used to store lobster at Bunker. Here the lobster stay fresh and lively for a long time. When lobsters are wanted, the pound keepers simply row a "scraper" out and detach the needed lobster from the bottom.

The pound master went on to complete my lobster lore: he described how lobster behave in the trap. Each trap is a rather elaborate construction of wood lathes and netting. It has two rooms; one is a small one open

to the sea, with net funnels which narrow at the interior end. The lobster crawls in the funnel to get at the bait ("well-aged" fish) in the bait bag hung at the middle of this first "room." When he gets inside, the lobster finds himself unable to break into the bag. All he gets is a smidgeon of the bait; enraged, he seeks to leave. The easiest way out is through another net funnel into the "living room," which takes up more than half the lobster trap. Once in, he finds it hard to get back out; here he stays. He has made space for new arrivals in the "entry hall."

" 'Course he can get back out if he has a mind to," said the pound master. "Don't believe a lobster would go in someplace he can't get out."

There were about ten active lobster boats in the harbor. The town sends out *100,000 pounds* of lobster a year! This means each lobster fisherman has to boat 10,000 pounds. If a couple of months time is allowed out for fixing traps, mending boats, "idle days" and a few other odd holidays it works out to thirty lobster a day a man. This way, town by town, 15,000,000 to 20,000,000 pounds of lobster a year are landed in Maine, taken from the amazing sea, so prodigal in its largess. One village like Bunker lands more lobster than is landed in the whole of Long Island Sound.

A lobster fisherman now came in from the outer harbor and proffered four fighting-mad lobster (they stretched their arms at right angles and made rapid pinching movements with their unpegged claws) for four dollars. We bought. We steamed them in thirty minutes over the alcohol flame simply by putting a half a quart of boiling water into the bottom of the bucket and lidding it.

Eating lobster *au Maine* is a sort of Roman thing. None of your baked-out, crumb-filled, nicely cut apart, hardly recognizable lobster that you can be—mistakenly—served in New York or even (I am ashamed to say it) in Maine. Proper lobster comes hot out of the bucket, and you do your own rending. Each claw leg is detached, the claws cracked with a "lobster cracker" (a hammer, gently pounded will do) and then the nectar of lobster slowly sipped out of the particular segment of shell before the meat is extracted.

So it went with us this evening. Each lobster went down segment by segment, until we were left with the small spiderlike hind legs which we slowly chewed to force the meat out; as a dessert (this is only for the real *aficionado*), the delicious mild green-tinted paste in the front of the body shell.

The above description does nothing to suggest the speed with which a dedicated lobster gourmand can turn the lobster into a hollow shell of its former self. Pat quit after we'd done three lobster together, leaving me to the fourth which I lovingly finished off by the light of the kerosene lamp. We let the shells softly and gratefully into the tide and retired to the slumber which comes as an inevitable and glorious aftermath to all happy, right-thinking lobster eaters.

*Friday, August 26.* A local shower spattered against the canvas top; it was another late and comfortable morning. The sky slowly cleared as the sea gulls settled on a ledge astern of us and sat with tucked wings, white puffballs patiently having a rest until the sun should come out and liven things up. The boat was hardly moving at all because the surge outside was killed by the barrier to the inner harbor.

A few children appeared on the banks, playing. Their voices could be heard shouting faintly among the houses. Otherwise there was complete peace. I began to think things like, "Now if I began to write fiction, I could leave New York, buy a house here cheap..." and so on.

We moved out of Bunker before noon for Birch Harbor, a small niche a bit to the north. We meant to have lunch here. We came into Birch on a bearing of 9 Magnetic from the can off Bunker Ledge. This is a bit roundabout, but there is no substitute for sailing from a known position and this can was the best point to take a bearing from. If I hadn't had my bearing to look to, I would probably have initially missed the not-easily-spotted mouth of Birch altogether, wasting any time that I had saved by shortcutting and coming in by the seat of my pants. I held 9 degrees and the harbor eventually opened up. I turned toward the southerly shore on account of a rock marked on the chart, on the north shore of the harbor. "Roaring Bull" sounded fierce enough (one of several Roaring Bulls along the coast, though) but it never put in an appearance in the mouth of the harbor while we sat there through low tide. Incidentally, this is what we might have expected, since the rock as marked on the chart is *not* circled with a ring of small dots. A ring specifies that a rock is definitely a menace to navigation.

*Granite, pine, water:*
*elements that have*
*exercised the same spell over*
*every sailor of these shores*

Birch is no longer a fishing harbor, contrary to what "The Bible" states, and does not have a gas dock, contrary to what the *Coast Pilot* states. It is only a very pleasant little summer-cottage harbor, with a small rock and pebble beach. It has ten feet at low tide almost all the way into the opening of the inner harbor. The inner harbor, however, dries out and I wouldn't go in there except to get out of a hellish blow. The surge coming in the outer harbor is somewhat more than at Bunker, but if you get far enough in it is not tiresome. As a dividend, the bottom is excellent holding: the Danforth digs in almost as if by suction.

The sky had been clearing and the sun was now blasting down full. As we finished lunch Pat had a little lunch nap and put another coating on her copper tan before we took off for Corea.

Corea is a great little fishing village; it needs only some commonsense navigation to get in. The rock formations at the entranceway are bleak and beautiful in a typical Down East seascape style; they are also avoidable, a desirable added quality. There is an extremely satisfying view of fishing piers and wharves as one is coming in the entrance; there are a couple of gas docks to choose from; the one at the left, going in, is nearest the grocery store. As we approached, two lobster buyers at this float were crating lobster for shipping. One was dipping a great net into the lobster car at the float and dumping squirmy piles of lobster into a crate. When the scales on which the crate sat showed 100 pounds of clawing bucking lobster bodies, the crate was closed and tossed into the water to await the arrival of the refrigeration truck. The lobster would go to Massachusetts packed in ice.

This was to be the last shipment from Corea for a while. A lot of the lobster were getting soft shells, becoming so-called shedders. (A shedder is very lean on meat and usually is not sold.) The men were banding the big claw with a rubber strip using a pair of banding pliers rather than pegging them. The next lobsters caught would be stored in the lobster car for a good spell to harden. "Might not ship them until January," said one lobster buyer. "We're going to speculate on them a bit." In other words, prices might go up. A lobster is of somewhat more solid material than a stock certificate; nevertheless, the lobster is subject to the same kind of thinking and manipulation. The simple act of a lobster fisherman hauling in lobster and selling it to you on a yacht can escalate, in the speculation process, to a complicated commodity transaction in which millions of live bodies are held like wheat futures. There is a great deal of worry and prayer-making in the lobster market when the middlemen are trying to maximize their profit.

Pat and I needed supplies. We got a ride from a friendly tourist who was "doing" the U.S. alone in a VW sedan, a young San Franciscan. It was a quarter mile to the grocery store, and it was a real old-fashioned, wood-counter board-floor store run by an old man and woman; the stock is scarcely the kind you get at the A & P in an average Smalltown, U.S.A., but it will do in a pinch. There were a couple of young lads sitting about, ready to go off, it seemed, "raking." In these parts this means raking blueberries in the blueberry bogs. One of the boys, the old man's grandson, quite possibly, promised the proprietor, "be back Saturday to give you a shave." As an advance against the shaving operation, the young man took an Eskimo pie out of the freezer; then he and his friends took off in an old Fleetwood Cadillac, bound for the bogs, leaving the old man to close the freezer top and mutter, "He never shut the closet yet."

On our way back the sun came out. Pat located a patch of blueberries at roadside near the float and stayed to pick them; I got the hull gassed up.

Corea is the hometown of Louise Dickenson Rich, who years ago wrote *We Took to the Woods*, which be-

came a national best seller; she has since written quite a bit on Maine, including the fine book *The Coast of Maine*. The man at the wharf said, "Since she wrote that book, lots of people come here just to see this place."

For my money, Bunker Harbor is a lot cosier and a more worthwhile stop, but Corea is definitely more Way Down East in appearance.

We decided to have lunch and go to Carrying Place Cove, a very protected and interesting harbor, the next long inlet east.

Carrying Place Cove in Dyer Bay is a part of one of the "doubles" on the SLIDE course. A double is a set of paired harbors where in one condition you take one harbor and, in another condition, the harbor next door. For instance, in Vinalhaven, you could take your

shallow-draft boat into The Basin or your deep-draft to Crockett's Cove up the shore just a bit. And at Merchant's Row in a southerly breeze, you anchor between Round Island and McGlathery; in a northerly, you anchor between Enchanted and Saddleback. In the present instance the paired harbors are Carrying Place Cove and Big Head off Bois Bubert in Pigeon Hill Bay. If there is a strong rolling surge from the south, you are best off taking the time to go into the massive protection of Carrying Place Cove. Otherwise, the most interesting route east is through Pigeon Hill Bay parallel the Bois Bubert shore (stay well out in the middle). Pigeon Hill Bay is, happily, open at both ends, so you avoid doubling back (Map Thirteen, page 168).

Today we had a really big surge: the rollers were running off the Gulf of Maine as if they couldn't wait to make harbor. And so we went racing along the spectacular line of seaward rocks across the mouths of Gouldsboro Bay and Dyer Bay, turned north at one sea-stained rock and sped three miles up Dyer.

The whole length of Dyer, like most of these long bays past Schoodic, contains fishing villages at every sizable bight of land. This part of the coast is where, undisturbed by tourists, a good portion of Maine's 15,000 lobster fishermen go hunting.

At Birch Point we turned around an islet into Carrying Place Cove, hunting the narrow channel with the Raytheon; since it was high tide, the fathometer served well to locate an anchorage that would still be wet at low. We got way in to the end of the first inlet, keeping well toward the left shore, and anchored about 120 feet offshore. Here we were able to swing in an arc with a safe twenty-foot reading all about. It was very well protected and quiet, exactly what we wanted.

In the deepening blue of the sky overhead as we swung at anchor, the moon came out three-quarters full and white, hardly showing any scars at all from frequent Russian and American hits. As Pat stirred up

*Past Schoodic, the Eastern coast begins*

dinner, the moon's surface turned bullion and struck down on the quiet water at the mouth of the tidal stream going inland from us. Now the place had the look, for all the world, of a quiet stretch of the Wabash River in the heart of Hoosier country. All that was missing was the new-mown hay. Instead, we had the warm scent of pine needles, their fragrance reminiscing on the heat of the day.

*Saturday, August 27.* Maine was favoring us with a run of glorious weather. Such runs used to be rarer but since the whole Northeast has had somewhat less rainfall in recent years, the farmers have had drought, but summer vacationists have had deeper tans. The sun stood up like a ball of fire over the dome of Pigeon Hill at the head of Carrying Place Cove. The cormorants and gulls were wheeling about looking early for breakfast in the quiet of the cove.

The farther east one gets the more cormorants one sees. Less elegantly, they are called shags (and still less elegant, the local name is "shitepokes"). These birds appear to be a cross between a gull and a small dirty pelican. You can easily tell them at a distance by their flight: they are smaller than the gull and never rest on their wings; they beat their way through the sky in stubby strokes which never seem to vary. Having alighted, they point their long beaks skyward as if to make up for small stature. And they have a strutting pose, a stance that consists of standing on tiptoe, wings extended as if posing for the top bird on a totem pole. In this pose they start fanning like the Pharisee beating his breast, but the bird is probably just getting rid of a kink in the neck.

We did a small exploration up the tidal river and into the upper reaches of Carrying Place Cove. It was over a mile from the end of the harbor where we lay to the head of the cave. I have a feeling that a six-foot-draft craft with a good fathometer could spend a day in here and chart a safe course at least another quarter of a mile in from our position to find a place big enough to anchor comfortably for the night. This would be all to the good, because the present head of navigation is in the middle of a swatch of lobster pots and even the most well-meaning of lobster fishermen is not going to quiet his motor to a mile-an-hour putter just to keep cruising people happy.

We explored via *X-ray* and Kinky, so it was a quick little jaunt down past the island in midstream to the head of the cove. At the end, the western outskirts of the town of Pigeon Hill were represented by a fisherman's shack and a boat pulled up above the tide line. Now we saw a cloud of duck taking off, then a species of geese. And then a lone heavy-flapping bird big as a heron, but without the trailing legs: an eagle.

Had I had time, I should have stayed to ferret out more of the cove's secrets. There is surely fresh water somewhere here and possibly a pond for swimming. I feel too little has been done to supply yachtsmen with knowledge of the lesser-frequented bays in Maine. I would say that the State of Maine might do well (I am an inveterate hypotheticist) to encourage yachtsmen to contribute their findings to a publication which the state could put out in loose-leaf form and update every year. There is a yachtsmen's organization which does this for the cruising territory in upper Lake Huron, and it works out very well.

As it stands now, the closest thing we have is D & B, "The Bible." For economic reasons, one cannot expect the publisher, Dodd, Mead, to revise and add to it each year. Nor can any small group of men explore the whole coast thoroughly. This is work for a legion of yachtsmen, cooperatively.

To get a close shot of *X-ray* and Kinky in action, I put Pat out on a small rock near the boat and she took pictures as I helmed. She looked so appealing on the rock, like that bronze mermaid that sits on a rock in

the harbor in Copenhagen, that I had to take a couple of shots of her as well.

It was time to move east again. We'd had our little fun. (I hope the reader will notice that I studiously follow my own advice and stay long enough at every stop to really enjoy it.)

We rounded to a noon course due south and headed out to sea. The day was partly clouded; the occasional shadings over the sun dropped the temperature considerably. Cruising this far east, for my money, is only worth it in good warm weather; if a siege of bad is predicted, one is better off to the west. Unless, of course, one simply adores long johns and Windbreakers. I get my fill of these skiing.

Now we crossed the famous Petit Manan Bar at the buoyed passage halfway out to Petit Manan Island. The lumpy and confused sea kept us going slowly and we had time to view the splendid spare needle of the Petit Manan light; to my mind this is the most perfect structure on the coast. I have sailed outside her: on a blustery day the noise and spray off the ledge on which she stands is awesome.

Incidentally the localization of the French-given name of Petit Manan is a glorious contraction, "Tit Nan." This reminds me of a favorite gripe. The names applied to the coast scenery through the ages have unfortunately sometimes been bowdlerized by the finickiness of the Coast and Geodetic Survey. Ragged Arse Island has simply become Ragged A. Island on their charts. This is a clear denial of the human spirit.

We laid a course for Cape Split where we'd stop for gas. We detoured inshore through Pigeon Hill Bay to pick up a much more interesting course rather than simply taking that outside. (See Map Thirteen, page 168.) We went past the town of Pigeon Hill (we were seeing the eastern side of it now) to port; almost exactly opposite, to starboard, Big Head on Bois Bubert. (How can you resist an island named Bois Bubert? On our return cruise we would stop here to explore Lily Pond.) Here, you stay out in the middle of Pigeon Hill Bay to avoid stakes from various fish weirs that occur nearer the shore.

Pat made En Route Sandwiches as we turned out of Pigeon Hill Bay and into the wilderness of islands at the bay's inner exit. Duncan and Blanchard is wary of this whole detour, but to us, the navigation and the scenery were pleasant and exciting. We sped by Pond Island beyond Bois Bubert; Pond's chalk-white abandoned light tower is for sale. (Ever wanted to buy an abandoned lighthouse in Maine? Here it is. Perfect location, solid construction, offered with adjoining structures, acres of surrounding woods, a guaranteed spray-creating cliff below and magnificent view.) We slid into Cape Split by three thirty and putted around for twenty minutes while lobster boats unloaded their catch at the one and only gas float. I had plenty of time, while waiting, to take in the harbor. I didn't find it as breathtaking as some have, certainly, but it is an acceptably spare and clean vista; a nice-looking village with a standard lobster fleet as a set piece in the foreground.

*Map 14: Bois Bubert to Roque Island*

1. SLIDE *course from Pigeon Hill Bay.*

2. *Trafton Island anchorage.*

3. *Course to the town of Millbridge.*

4. *Flat Bay anchorage.*

5. *Harrington River anchorage.*

6. *Dyer Island anchorage.*

7. *Night Cap Island anchorage.*

8. *Pleasant River anchorage.*

9. *Cape Split. Fishing village and well-protected harbor.*

10. *Wohoa Bay anchorage.*

11. *Indian River anchorage.*

12. *Indian River Crossing. Head of a dinghy run, where groceries and beer are available at the bridge over Indian River.*

13. *Outside course to Head Harbor and Roque Island.*

14. *Continuation of the course to Head Harbor from the southwest corner of Great Wass Island.*

15. *Jonesport in Moosabec Reach; landing on the west side of the bridge to Beals.*

16. *Beals, town landing, off Moosabec Reach.*

17. *Jonesport. Look wharves and lobster pound, gas float, at the eastern end of Jonesport.*

18. *The Ranges. Course along marked channel out to harbors on Great Wass, Steele Harbor Island, and Head Harbor Island.*

19. *Crow Point Head anchorage, Head Harbor Island.*

20. *Mistake Harbor, Steele Harbor Island. Coast Guard station, moorings.*

21. *Sand Cove, Great Wass Island. A small anchorage off a perfect little beach.*

22. *Mud Hole, Great Wass Island. A narrow secluded gunkhole with great protection.*

23. *Head Harbor, Head Harbor Island.*

24. *Cows Yard, off Head Harbor. A place beloved of the yachtsmen who seek the special.*

25. *Course from Moosabec Beach to Roque Island.*

26. *Roque Island. Beach anchorage: the most beautiful anchorage on the coast; a mile of wide sand beach.*

27. *Roque Island. Weir anchorage at the west end of Roque beach.*

28. *Bunker Cove. One of the snuggest of Maine anchorages.*

29. *Roque Island Thorofare. Route to the west and north shores of the island.*

30. *Shorey Cove. North shore of Roque.*

31. *Lakeman Harbor. Another Roque anchorage.*

32. *Roque Bluff anchorage.*

33. *Course to Machias River and Machias. A city on the river. Also the course to the Maine coast around Passamaquoddy.*

This is a planning aid; use only U.S. Geodetic charts for navigation.

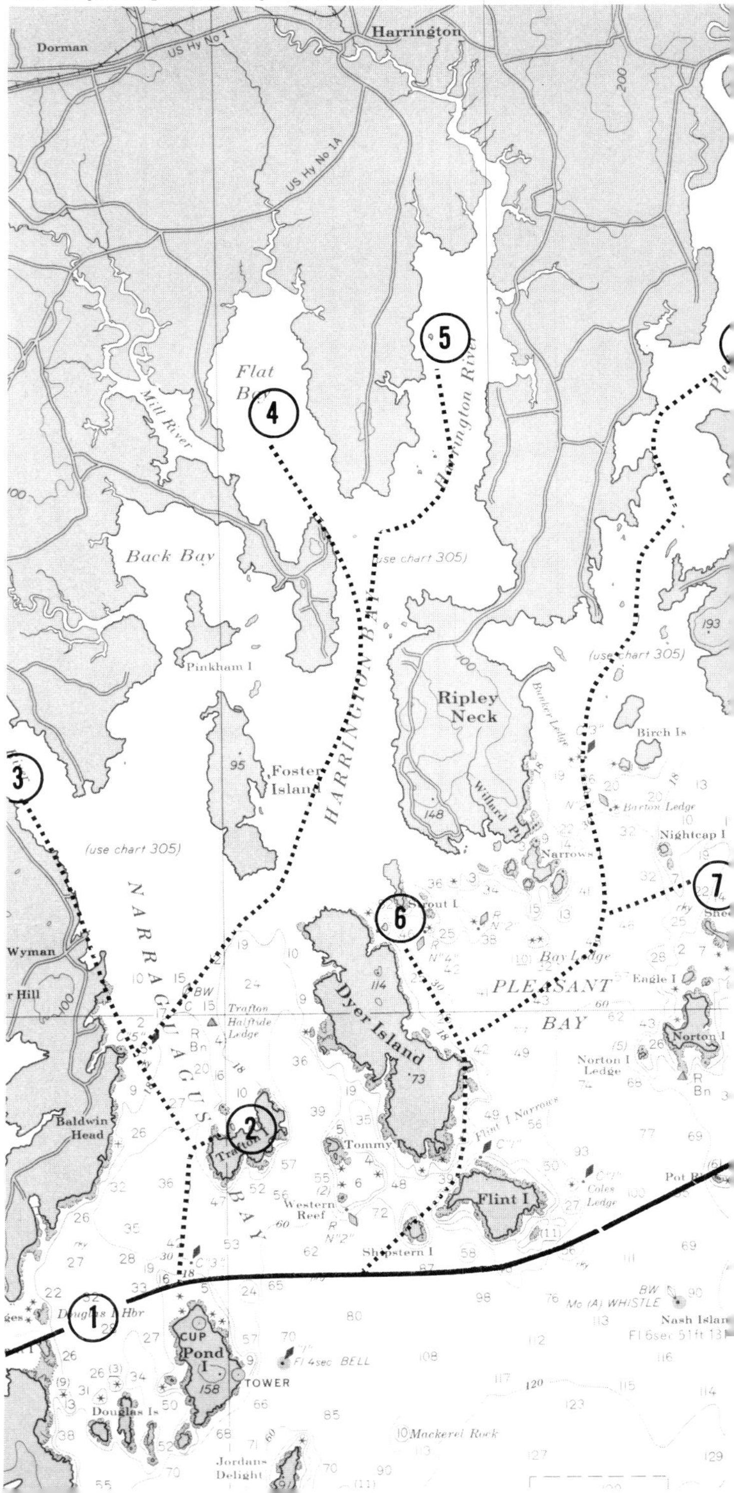

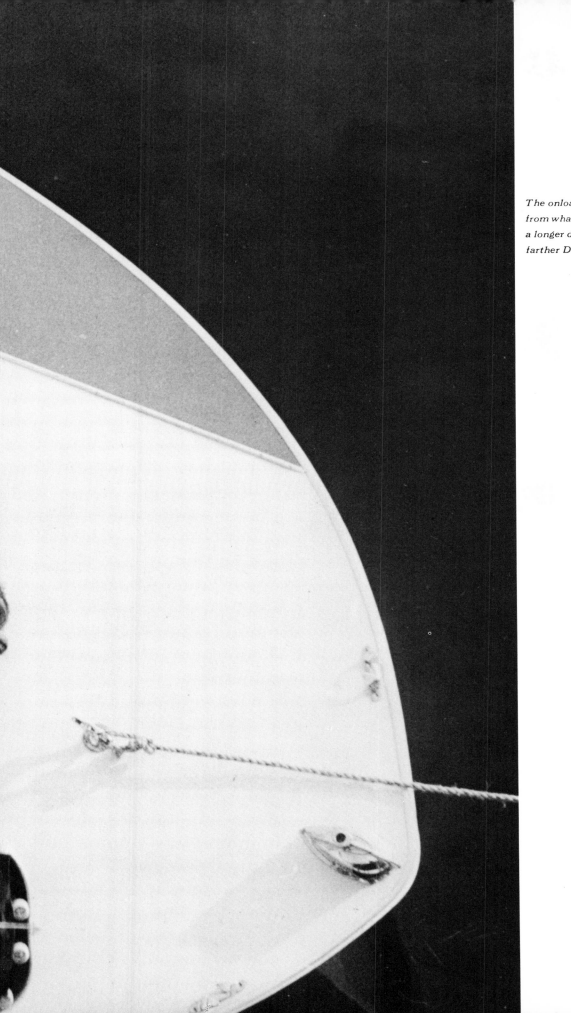

*The onloading of goods
from wharves gets to be
a longer drop the
farther Down East it is*

Over at one side of the harbor, a larger fishing vessel was careened on shore for repair. The tide may be a nuisance or a fascination to yachtsmen but to the fisherman it is his readily available, absolutely free hydraulic lift; he can run his craft into a cradle and let the tide fall away so that his hull sits upright for repair; he can also run the hull up on a smooth stretch and have her careen (lie over on her side) if that is more convenient. When repairs are over, the sea obligingly takes his hull back again. No charge.

A lobster fisherman at the float who saw me circling invited us to tie alongside his craft. I accepted reluctantly because the lines of a yacht and of a lobster boat do not match well. It took a bit of doing to raft our hulls without damage, requiring all kinds of bumpers between the hulls.

The grocery ashore near the wharf was a cut above the one at Corea, but it lacked all vegetables and meat. Gas, of course, at the float, and water from a well at the top of the hill. No ice or liquor. A man offered to take us into South Addison where more magnificent stocks of groceries were available—it would take about fifteen minutes each way. We thanked him and said we'd try farther on at Jonesport; we were anxious to get to this gateway to a really sumptuous cruising territory. The islands just outside Jonesport and the islands in Chandler's and Englishman's Bays are superb.

As I was taking on gas, I asked a lobster fisherman on the float if the lobstering was getting any better.

"Poorah," he said.

"Too bad," I said.

"Gets any worse, don't know what we'll do. Have to go somewhere, I guess. Don't know where, though. Lobster is all we got."

He was a gloomy Hamlet among lobster fishermen but nevertheless, he had a point. The farther east you get, the truer it is that the flow of lobster from the bottom of the sea to the van of the refrigerator trucks represents the total flow of the economic lifeblood of the towns.

Onward to Jonesport. (See Map Fourteen, page 184.) We soon spotted the rainbow arch of the bridge over Moosabec Reach at Jonesport. This structure has spoiled the Reach for most sailing vessels who must now take the outside course to the islands. Now to port we had the gray shacks of the "suburbs" of "West Jonesport" and to starboard the town of Beals. Once through the piers of the bridge, we were off the middle of Jonesport proper with its proper houses. We steered down to the spire of the Congregational church where stood the high pilings of the Look lobster establishment. There is no float at any pier near shore and the pilings looked to be very rough-surfaced; I dropped a stern anchor on the way in to the inside gas pier and tied bow-to at one of the wood ladders. It was a good fifteen-foot climb up the ladder to the deck of the wharf. Pat, who claims to have acrophobia, had been training on longer and longer ladders all the way up the coast and she made this one all right, too. We found one grocery store by walking past the Congregational church (a pretty one) and taking a right on the main road when we came to it. It was about a twenty-minute walk to the Emerson grocery, in the same building as the Emerson garage. It was a good bit above the one at Cape Split, but had no fresh meats or vegetables.

The son of the very kind proprietor here consented to take us "over the border," seven miles away, to Indian River in South Addison Township: here, at the head of tidewater in Indian River there was a grocery store with *beer!* The grocery which sold beer was a good one, we found, but again had nothing fresh except fruit. If a thirsty yachtsman with shoal-draft hull were to navigate Indian River at high tide, he could anchor in midstream and dinghy in to the bridge on the Indian River where this store lies.

We also found a second grocery store in Jonesport

which did have fresh meat and a few fresh vegetables. To get to this by boat you would moor at the Coast Guard station by the huge aluminum towers just west of the Moosabec bridge or the commercial dock just east of it (both would require permission). The grocery is just up the road that leads off the bridge. Ice: you have to drive fourteen miles out of town to Columbia Falls to get crushed ice at the ice-making plant.

The reason for my emphasis on information about supplies is that good supplies are scarce once you leave Mount Desert. Knowing where to get them becomes more valuable the farther east you go.

It was pretty obvious to us, riding around, that Jonesport men have had it hard counting on lobster for a living. One sardine plant (where the Coast Guard station now is) has moved its machines to Southwest Harbor. The town's peat moss industry has died. The center of town is full of empty stores and offices. Lobster can't do it all.

We lowered our hard-won supplies from the pier to the deck of the ship by bucket and line. Pat, on deck below, was handing in the bucket when one whole beer —a tenth of our supply—toppled into the salt water. Tragedy! While Pat stowed groceries, I attempted to retrieve the beer. I cast the tin bucket on a line and let it drop to the bottom. As I dragged for the bottle, the chimes in the Congregational church struck up "Rock of Ages." They were excellent bells, soft and melodious, and their spell was cast (Jonesport is a dry town, remember, and nothing is more pervasive than the dryness of a Congregational dry town). I missed snaring my bottle, miserable sinner I. The silt stirred up and the bright Narragansett label disappeared from view.

I now charted the rather intricate course of the side trip from Jonesport for the delightful passage out to Head Harbor and the Cows Yard (see Map Fourteen, page 184). I took the Congregational spire as a mark

and ran a course from that out to Nun 14. As we left for the somewhat delicate crossing to Head Harbor, the Congregational chimes played "The Old Rugged Cross." With the nuns to guide us, we set off.

Whether divine guidance or no, the trip was not as rugged as it looked on the chart and this is all to the good. Taken as a whole, there is probably no more beautiful bit of coast country of similar size than that right off Jonesport. It is a series of smaller and larger islands with gay-hued fishing houses of the town of Beals strung along both sides of the channel and small islets with lone vacation shacks on them and perfect blue passages between; it is the only place that I've seen to compare with the skerries and reefs of the southern Norwegian coast. It is simply a perfect proportion of houses, land, and water; a new and more deft composition meets you at every bend.

There are shortcuts into Head Harbor and the Cows Yard, but I doubt if they are as enchanting as the buoyed course which takes you out the deep-water cut between Knights Island and Steele Harbor Island past the Moose Peak Coast Guard Station Light on Mistake Island and right on to the open sea. You then turn east and duck back into Head Harbor, fleeing the surge that swells up the line of pink rock that marks the end of land. Beyond is the Atlantic horizon.

The Cows Yard is the "inside harbor" of Head Harbor; it is a gorgeous circle of blue, large enough for a number of yachts to swing, set in islands and shores as green as Ireland's. There are two or three vacation cottages here; if you're as lucky as we were, you will be sole possessor of as superb a piece of watery real estate as you will see on the coast.

We charcoaled fresh ground beef, ate a welcome supper, and crawled into quick extinction of consciousness. As I was dozing off, I saw, out the window, a mainsail come sliding by the boat. Some real tough sailor was making the Cows Yard by moonlight.

*The town of Beals from*
*The Ranges, off Jonesport*

SUNDAY, AUGUST 28. Dawn over the Cows Yard. Off our stern rode a pretty, yachty thirty-five-footer with reverse sheer that belonged to the true blue sailor who'd made port late last night. Hewing close to my conception of him, he was up with the sun, catching the fresh-water condensation on deck in time to use his long-handled swab on it and clean the salt off his decks. He went below and soon came up with his family. They had eaten and checked out by nine o'clock, headed east. By god, now there was a sailing man.

We had a more leisurely program. It included sitting in the sun and listening to the unique rills of the tide in the Cows Yard; it always drums light watery fingers on any hull parked here. The turbulence in this anchorage is not of a spectacular frothing kind but it is nevertheless strong, as evidenced by the way the anchor line trembles like a violin string when you hand it out.

We had intended to go ashore to do some walking because the country to the east looked inviting but I had picked up a slight infection in the heel from a splinter on the pier at Looks' in Jonesport, so I took some polycillin to help the body fight the bad guys, sprayed antiseptic on the sore area, and bandaged it.

Across the island maze to Sand Cove is one of the most intriguing passages you can make but, unless you are planning to spend a week familiarizing yourself with the several hundred ledges, it is a very good idea to try to stick as much as possible to a route you have carefully charted, using the natural features as reference points. Trying to feel your way around without such courses will drive you to distraction.

We were fascinated: no matter which way you run here between Mistake Harbor and Great Wass Island on which Sand Cove lies, the rocks and ledges and islets break the water into photogenic straits through which the tide runs merrily; the surge breaks on rocks awash all over and it is very pretty *if only you know where you are in here.*

We saw our first sea pigeons of the trip. These are energetic little birds with a pair of white-banded wings which move at such a whirr that they appear to be king-size hummingbirds. They fly in close formation usually and, since their wings blur, your first impression is of a string of pale blue pearls buzzing across your line of vision. Should you come across them as they are paddling about on the surface, they'll go under with an energetic hop-and-duck motion that is reminiscent of cute kids diving in at the old swimming hole.

Sand Cove is a beautiful little place; it is perhaps seventy-five to a hundred yards wide just inside the reefs protecting the mouth. Here the harbor narrows down to a U-shape; there is a gravel beach at the bottom of the U with a ten- to twelve-foot strip of perfect white beach sand above high tide.

We found out that one should favor the starboard side of the cove going in, as a look at the lobster pot lineup told us. The rock sketchily marked on chart 305 was really a very considerable ledge and it was located two-thirds of the way over across the cove to our port: it reached inward from a point about a quarter of the distance of the whole length of the bay. Also, it had a mass of kelp growing on it, which made it easy to spot, for the kelp formed a dark purplish patch in the water. We motored straight in to the ten-foot reading on a fathometer at low tide and dropped anchor with plenty of room to swing.

Now we dinghied in to the sand and pulled *X-ray* up. For the next few hours we did nothing but lie blissfully prone and soak up enough heat to ward off all future chill, come less agreeable days.

After a couple of hours, we went back to our craft which was hobby-horsing about on the end of her nylon tether, frightened by the emerging ledge south of her. We went back to the buoyed course and carefully

out to sea again. I got turned around in here once and brazening my way out cost me many palpitations from "kelp readings" of two and three feet on the fathometer.

Roque Island was next.

Everyone talks so much about Roque that it may seem a bit disappointing at first look. The harbor is too big to be cozy, and you haven't been on the beach yet. But there it is, that fabulous generous strip of white gleaming sand, as fine and clean as on any exclusive cabanaed beach. Once you run in toward the beach, the ambience at Roque is that of a tropical lagoon. With a few palms you could play *South Pacific* here.

Some yachtsmen prefer to anchor in a small cove, Lakeman Harbor, an arm of Roque. There was, in fact, a sailboat in there as we motored in. But I prefer, unless there is a hell of a surge, to anchor right on the beach. The beach slopes down so steeply that you can put your bow on it unless you have a considerable keel. There is great holding ground here; the restful melodious roll of small waves on the sand shore is a fine lullaby of an evening.

Such was the effect the evening *Puff TMD* settled down off Roque Beach as her crew started the fires going for the evening meal. It was an evening of pure relaxed enjoyment. At the far end of the mile-long strip of beach our yachty friend from the Cows Yard was parked inside the picturesque fish weir west of the beach. And yet, only halfway down the beach from him, we had what can be classed as complete privacy, so far separated from him were we. Counting a small auxiliary anchored off the slate cliff formation east of the beach, we were four yachts in Roque that evening, and yet we had all the elbow room needed.

After we had had dinner, a nearly full moon came up between the two heads of Double Shot Island at the mouth of the harbor to perfect our landfall.

*Monday, August 29.* Roque is owned by the Gardner family. One of them, C. Peabody Gardner, has been an inveterate cruising man; he has written a book about Down East cruising called *Ready About* (A. S. Barnes, New York). The whole Gardner family is kindly disposed toward cruising people and amenable to having you go ashore and walk about on the beach and explore woods. You can rack out on the sand in your sleeping bag, if you wish. But the one thing you must not do is start any kind of fire ashore or smoke in the woods. There is no earthly way of putting out a forest fire on this island. The rule is honored strictly by all of us who make free of the island in other ways. A fire which marred Roque would be a national tragedy. Roque is one place whose features are not duplicated, nor ever will be, the length of the Atlantic coast.

In *Ready About*, Peabody Gardner tells of the three hermits who once lived on Little Spruce—an extension of Roque's western arm. The hermits were Daniel, William, and Nehemiah, all brothers. Gardner describes them as a hairy bearded triumvirate. As things stood with them, Daniel and William refused to speak to each other. They communicated through Nehemiah.

And Nehemiah was a minnesinger *manqué*. Although he could neither read nor write, he recited poems and sang—in a fine tenor—ballads he had composed and memorized. Hermit William once retired to his cabin for several years, insisting that sunshine leaking into the brain would cause same to explode if brought too near to the stove. Hermit Daniel built a crazy little yacht for himself called *Catch Me If You Can*. One good psychiatrist could have spoiled all this.

And on our second day on Roque, we woke to the

The arc of the beach at Roque Island

*The arc of the beach at Roque Island*

nicely tempered notes of the waves playing a soft tim-pani on the beach. Ball of Fire, old Sol, rose promptly at six. In order to spend the morning walking the beach, we took *Puff's* bow onto the shore. I dropped an anchor on the way in and now took the bow anchor up the beach a short distance and tied the free end of the stern anchor line to it. This line was simply looped through the cleat on the stern quarter of the craft. All we had to do then was to give *Puff* a push and she glided out along the line and hung there, moving back and forth with the surge. When we wanted something from the hull, we simply pulled her in by the bow line. A push and she returned obediently to her offshore position. With this arrangement we happily spent the whole day on the beach without having to use the dinghy.

At the east end of the beach there were some great slate cliffs, a change from the granite that is usual on the islands. It was a simple matter to climb the sand slides and get into the woods fifty or so feet above water. From the woods Roque Beach is a fairytale scene: a great scimitar of sand curving off to the hills on the other side and, within this arc, dancing blue water and a yacht. It is one of the most peaceful spots on earth.

In the afternoon we took the two-track path that curves off the western part of the beach to wander through Roque's thick jungle-like forest toward the northern shore at Shorey Cove. We glimpsed the Gardner place on the western arm of the cove and came back with the feeling of having seen hidden cities.

The beach is one place where the lobster fishermen don't come, presumably because lobsters and sand don't mix. In the twenty-four hours that we spent here, only four cruising auxiliaries came in and left. One departure was our friend from the Cows Yard; he left at noon the first day, doubtless ashamed of having been caught idling about for half a day when he could have

been strapped down, rail-under at sea.

We now had a week to get back. I could have stretched a point and gone east for another day; but truth is, one must go way, way Down East—all the way to Quoddy Head and the bays around Eastport or up the St. John's River or alternatively into the tidal lakes of Nova Scotia—before one can better the cruising grounds off Jonesport. To include a few more ports farther up the eastern coast would have been to devalue the experiences that we'd already had. I didn't want to knock our cruise in the head by making our last week an endurance race back.

We took the "inside route" out of Roque by leaving the magic harbor via Roque Thorofare. We went through this close "pirate-country" passage just astern of a beautiful light blue Hinckley auxiliary which turned off into Bunker Cove to anchor. Bunker Cove is navigable at high tide all the way through to a far exit; this, the tiny passage of Bunkers Hole, is where Captain Bunker, pursued by the British during the Revolutin, hid his schooner, chopped her masts, felled some trees across her deck, and then escaped in a skiff. The British found neither Bunker nor boat. The place has been Bunkers Hole ever since.

From Bunker Cove to Chandler's Bay outside Roque was but a minute's work for us. We soon closed on Moosabec Reach, meeting the line of welcoming nuns doing a grave nodding dance in the stiff chop. *Puff* sped on, bouncing and spreading her wide white wings of spray at each crest.

We pulled up to O. W. and B. S. Look's Jonesport wharves; the long-legged structures now were standing so far out of water that in the blinding backlight of the sun they looked like an army of telephone poles in a flooded land.

I had to wait for gas until a refrigerator truck was loaded by the wharfmen: lobsters come first. I stood about easily and talked with the winch operator and

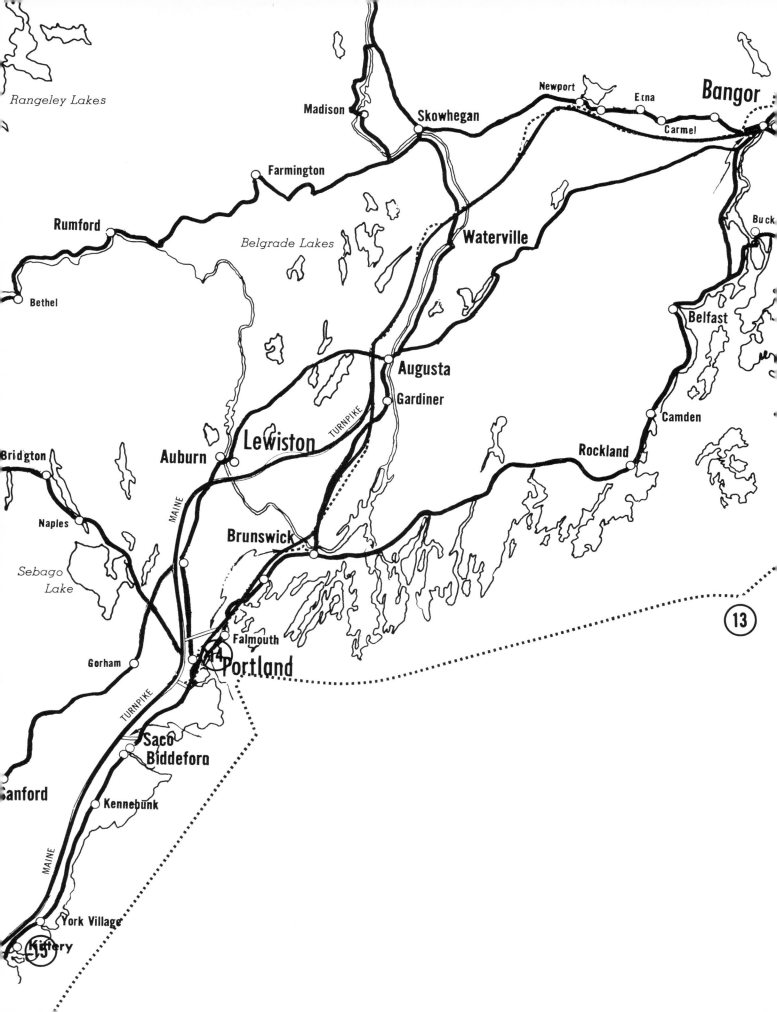

*Medd.*
*Lake*

own

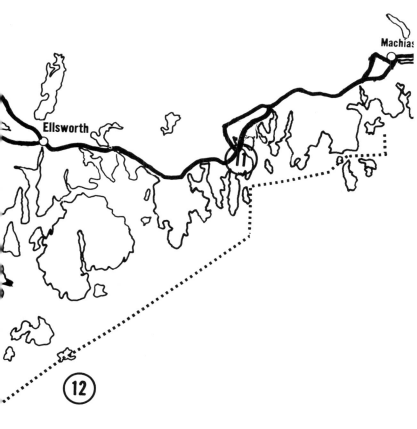

Machias

Ellsworth

⑪

⑫

*Map 15: Return Cruise: Five Days West'ard*

*The return cruise starts at Roque Island on the tenth day:*

11. *Pigeon Hill and Carrying Place Cove. On your first day back you can pick: go through Pigeon Hill Waters and if it's calm, stay. If not, go to the next reach down: Dyer Bay and go in as far as Carrying Place Cove.*

12. *Frenchboro and Swans Island: pick either the old fishing town of Frenchboro in Lunts Harbor on Long Island or go across the way to Burnt Coat Harbor on Swans Island.*

13. *Matinicus, Criehaven and Monhegan: Matinicus and its port on the sister island of Ragged—Criehaven— is only a short jump from Frenchboro. You may want to go on to anchor at Monhegan if the weather promises exceptionally fair going; otherwise stay in the marvelous isolated harbor town of Matinicus.*

14. *Falmouth Foreside. Here in Casco Bay you have the choice of leaving your yacht at Handy Boat Service and flying back from Portland to return for your boat later; or of going on to Kittery and exiting from Maine via water during your vacation.*

15. *Kittery: last stop in Maine. You have one more day of your sixteen-day vacation to get to home port.*

This is a planning aid: use only U.S. Geodetic charts for navigation.

*On the beach: Roque Island*

watched the truculent lobsters' last ride begin as the lobster crates were snatched out of the water below by the winch and swung into the wide-open door of the truck.

A small mongrel was having himself a great game: he would attack each crate with his teeth and give it a good bite as it cleared the edge of the wharf and another nip as it swung toward the truck doors. Once the dripping crate was in the truck, the dog would stand under the truck body between the rear wheels and dance madly about in a circle, nipping at the drops of water that came splattering through the cracks.

By the time we'd gotten our gas mixed and into the tanks it was dark; we tied our bow to the wharf and dropped a stern anchor with just enough line to keep us off at low tide; we swung off Jonesport in a very quiet evening.

I'd wish for the Jonesport-Beals area, though, some sort of yachting establishment to compare with Manset's Hinckley. There are plenty of cruising people going by here and this is equal, as a cruising ground, to Penobscot or Mount Desert. The town of Beals on Beals Island has more charm than any town on the Penobscot; the cruising, if somewhat different, is all the more exciting for that. But the rounds you have to make to collect groceries, supplies, and ice cuts down the time you can spend cruising.

Beals Island has a long and illustrious shipbuilding reputation. If a proper marina were to be set up there, very possibly some sort of yacht building comparable to Hinckley's could bloom as a result. There is no reason why Jonesport-Beals could not be a great way station on any cruise Down East.

*Tuesday, August 30.* The morbid intermittent tones of foghorns blowing on the coast, answering each other and saying in funereal monotone " 'Tis true! 'Tis true!" woke the crew of *Puff* this day at Jonesport. The fog lay in as thick as paste, sticking to structures and pilings like white glue. "A high intensity fog, I see," I said calmly, pulling my head in from outside the curtain of the cockpit cover and falling back on my sleeping bag. An hour or so later Pat swung a censer of coffee under my nose and I bestirred myself and looked out the shimmering plastic windowpanes. Someone had put a dirty wool carpet smack across both panes. "Thick o'fog this morning, eyuh," I said and reached for my heroin needle.

The sun finally but feebly surmounted the high walls thrown up by the fog at about ten o'clock, shining through with wan demeanor, like an orphan's face pressed against a store window. And that way it stayed for a while.

My heel hadn't responded to antibiotics very rapidly and was, in fact, getting swollen. I had intended to check with a doctor in Southwest Harbor. Now I decided that as long as the fog was holding, I'd try Jonesport. We went up to the O. W. and B. S. Look office inside the building on the wharf and were offered the use of the phone by Sid, my friend on the winch from the night before. I found out that the only doctor in Jonesport was in Texas for his daughter's wedding and that the nearest doctors were in Machias, so I called one of them. Sure, if I could get there, he'd look at me. We got a Jonesport lad to agree to drive us to Machias, twenty miles off. While we waited for him to appear with car, a very natty individual, Bert Look, came in and sat down at the desk opposite us; he started to conduct business at a great rate. The Looks seem to have quite a few things going for them here: movie houses, dances, oil business, and a few other things besides lobsters. Bert had close-cut black hair streaked with gray, wore a white shirt and tie, and seemed to be on top of everything all at once, from selling lobsters to showing *The Ten Commandments*.

He explained he had a big lobster pound up on Deer

Isle in New Brunswick: the water was colder up there and you could keep lobster indefinitely. Down here, where the pound held only 30,000 as compared to 300,000 in New Brunswick, "you can only keep lobster so long."

I remarked that it was a pity that there weren't a few more conveniences for yachtsmen here. Bert said that this was so and that while more and more yachts were coming through, right now the situation was that there weren't enough yachts to keep a marina going, whereas Hinckley had a couple of hundred yachts just sitting there all the time. "If there were enough yachts, we'd have a marina," said Bert.

I said that if they had a marina there might be enough yachts. "You'd spend fifty thousand dollars and sit around waiting," said Bert. I suggested that if someone invested $5,000 in a float which held a shower, a pay phone, an ice-vending machine, and a water hose, yachtsmen would be happy. Bert allowed that $5,000 wouldn't build much on the waterfront these days.

By this time our car for Machias had arrived and we were off. We were driven over rolling hills past fields where the crews were raking blueberries. Berry fields are burnt over to rid them of the green stuff, and the berries, which remain, are raked in like grass. The lad who drove us said that the rakers got $3.50 a bushel and that you could rake at least a bushel an hour or more. Some rakers took home $15 a day. I said they must take home some sore muscles too. "The first day is the worst," said our driver. "After that you're all right."

The doctor proved to be a sport. He had a Goldwater campaign sign on his front door and Goldwater's biography on the waiting room shelf. He bustled out, a sturdy square-built fellow with glasses. "Cruising, eh? Like it? Good. Let's see that foot. Aha, doesn't hurt me a bit," he said as he scissored off a chunk of skin. "Got to open her up," he explained. "What are you doing

*A crew is to work*

cruising when you should be shooting Johnson and other criminals like that? I got a twenty-square-foot poster of him that I use for target practice."

"Ah-ah-ah—" I said. I tried to pull my foot back.

"Just a minute now. Didn't get all of that splinter out yet." He waved around about an inch of wood that I had been carrying in my foot. "Ou-ou-ou," I said.

"Quick shot," said the doctor and stabbed me with a needle in the arm. "Could be a nasty infection with that thick skin to keep it in. Know what? I think Kennedy's still alive. I've read enough to convince me now. Tippit was shot in the same place, see?"

"Now the tetanus, other arm." He stabbed again. "Take these pills, four a day, use this salve, soak it in water for thirty minutes when you are having your drink at night."

"I'll vote against Medicare," I said thankfully as the pain started to leave my heel.

"No. No. Vote for it. The quicker we go to rack and ruin and start over, the better."

When we got back, the lady who worked in the Look office asked how it had gone. I said fine, as I sat down wearily. "Nice looking dog you have there," I said. She said yes, it was, and he was big even for a Newfoundland. He was called Big John and he was a town character. Yes, she said, he likes to shop. He also likes to

play with the tame harbor seal that comes in to the wharves here. The seal was raised by a fisherman and he still hangs about wharves and comes in every day to watch the people at Looks' while they work on the lobster cars. It sure is a sight to see him and Big John playing out in the water. I said yes, it must be, and that I had had a visit from the seal that very morning (which I had had) and that I had *thought* it was unusual to see a seal swimming so close off the stern of the boat, but then, you see everything in a fog.

As it happened, the seal had played like a big happy puppy dog and it seemed perfectly natural that he should be swimming and blowing his breath out noisily six inches from the propellers.

So, if you stop at Jonesport, dear reader, I hope you'll remember a dog playing tag with a seal out in the water between the lobster cars at Jonesport is perfectly natural.

On my way to the boat I stopped to inspect a bucket of huge snails in the back of a green pickup truck on the wharf.

"What are they?" I asked the driver.

"Conkles," said the driver.

"What do you do with them?" I asked.

"Eat them," said the driver.

I offered to buy some. The driver said, "Take as many as you want. No market for them anyway." And he trotted off on business. I turned to an old lobster fisherman who was standing by and asked him if conkles tasted good. "Sure do. Little tough, but tasty. Cook 'em in fresh water twenty minutes or so and if you can pull them out of the shell easy with a fork, they're ready."

"Could you cook them in seawater?"

The old lobster fisherman thought for a while. "Don't see why not," he said. "But they taste good cooked in fresh water for sure."

So I took about twenty conkles with me together

From Bois Bubert's shore
at Big Head, looking
across to Pigeon Hill Bay

with further instructions for supping off conkles, to wit: wash them in salt water, after cooking, pull off both the tail and the hard "nose." A little salt and lemon juice and pop 'em in.

As a footnote, let it be said that conkles evidently get into lobster traps in some waters in great numbers and quite a few fishermen eat them to vary their heavy-on-lobster diet, even though conkles are not a "commercial" shellfish. The conkle, I found out later, is a "waved whelk" and one of several of the whelks on our coast.

So conkle-whelks and all, Pat and I took off for the west.

By 4 P.M. we were cruising West'ard headed toward Pigeon Hill Bay (Map Fourteen, page 184).

First, we scooted out of Moosabec and hightailed toward Big Nash Island. It was soon five thirty but given a good smooth sea we could do with *Puff* what would be a day's sail in an auxiliary, and do it between five and dinnertime.

Out into Wohoa Bay, the swell turned to a stiff chop, and we had to come down from fifteen or sixteen to about six. We cut for Pigeon Hill and came running through the rollers in Flint Island Narrows and into Douglas Island Harbor and finally through Pea Narrows (love that name) to Pigeon Bay itself. Pigeon Bay, contrary to reputation, gives pretty good protection against the southerly roll and the westerly chop we had had. The trick is to anchor opposite the town of Pigeon Hill, north of the red shingle house on Bois Bubert. This is north of the fish weir stake area; if you proceed cautiously for the last hundred yards you can anchor blind almost anywhere here.

We splashed the Danforth gratefully in and got the fires going. We were the only yacht in the bay as far as I could see. The friendly lights of the town of Pigeon Hill, strung along the shore west of us, let us know we were welcome.

*Frenchboro town, Lunts Harbor, Long Island*

WEDNESDAY, AUGUST 31. We decided to spend a day in Pigeon Hill exploring Bois Bubert, looking for a freshwater pond that is located on the chart. Taking *X-ray* in to the beach, we put her painter between two big stones and left her. We asked a boy on the beach how to get to the pond. He said that there was a path up through the woods, fairly well trod. We took his directions and went back of a yellow house to find the path. The woods along the path were thick and bosky; the temperature was ten degrees warmer than at sea. We footed up and up for about thirty minutes and then the track petered out at a second bald granite rock clearing on top. I knew that the chart showed the highest hill, Big Head, to be north and east of the pond so I plunged boldly through the brush to the south and west: lo, there it was, a perfect blue circle shining through the slits in the green spruce fir.

Someone had built a small pier out into the pond from the west shore. The bottom is fairly soft, having been undisturbed for years. Green needles and leaves settled softly through the water and slowly decayed, leaving many feet of silt there.

But the pier led out to a five-foot depth of good sweet water. Having foresightedly brought soap and towels, we proceeded to have a fine bath, rinsing by diving off the end.

Locally, this is called the Lily Pond; there were lots of the green lily pads about but we'd come too late for the bloom. I am sure that they are spectacular in bloom. This was an authentic Thoreau pond. There are no people, no cottages, only woods paths sneaking in and out, a few minnow in the dark shadows of the water, and stillness; we could hear the distant sound of surf over the hush.

We came back refreshed to the beach and went hunting for a spring that we had heard about. We went along the path past the front of the red shingle house, then walked it parallel to the shore and across a field and then followed it down into alder bushes. About twenty feet in, we found a wooden trough and a spring. The water was delicious. While we waited for our bottles to fill, we sat up in the field and looked out over the bay; the sun warmed steadily and the grass smelled like grass should in summer.

Water bottled, ourselves well washed, we got back on *Puff* after two hours ashore, ready for more miles at sea.

After lunch, we—intrepid duo—left flying for Lunts Harbor on Long Island, about thirty nautical miles from our anchorage. We were now on our SLIDE return course, which island-hops in order to give the straightest possible course back to Portland and Kittery. (See Map Fifteen, page 194.)

Our first course was 200 on the compass out toward Petit Manan light; we ran under a high ceiling of cumulus clouds sailing overhead like servings of heaped white sherbet. Waves were breaking white all along Petit Manan Bar which slanted from the "Tit Nan" light outside of us to Gouldsboro Bay inside.

Some day they'll buoy the inner passage for vacation sailors, but until then taking the buoyed outer passage saves time compared to feeling your way over the inner bar with fathometer. Also, if the sea is making, the inner passage can be an unpleasantly rough bit of action. It has been known to shake masts loose.

You are very seldom without a few ledges to watch on the coast, even when going "outside" as we were doing. There is something stirring and elemental, adducing a note of subdued savagery, in seeing water and rock meeting forcibly in an arena of sea. At Moulton Ledges, the sea rose in a great bulge of power, gathering itself for a huge assault; it broke down over the ledge in a curl of white, a show of glittering fangs. As the ledge disappeared under a white avalanche, a smoky plume exploded skyward, signaling the destruction of the ledge but no! the plume subsided and the waters parted,

*Furling the main, Lunts Harbor*

revealing the ledge, dripping from battle yet unsubdued. And the sea rises again and again and falls on its enemy. Each time it produces a sound like the shock of armies meeting in battle, a reverberation which you feel in your bones. Each ledge and each tide has its own variation of this battle.

The noise has given rise to many reefs with names such as Thumper, Thrumcap, Roaring Bull, and the like. But there are better-named reefs. For instance, I prefer the more sprightly Nipple.

We now passed outside Schoodic Island, a more spectacular passage than the one inside. The end of Schoodic Island was throwing a huge boiling spray cloud that billowed constantly as if the land's end were burning. Here we met again the baby blue Hinckley from Bunker Cove; it was tacking slowly, moving against the tide in a light wind. We slowed down and went astern as is polite (and appreciated) and got a wave from the crew.

We then went spinning over hill and dale, our twin forties singing in happy synchronization as the Gale speedometer read "Fifteen . . . sixteen . . . seventeen . . . sixteen" to show us that we were properly trimmed and everything was pulling for speed. (X-ray was stashed on the forward deck, stuck cleverly out to one side so she didn't block the driver's view.)

After Schoodic, we were off Mount Desert. The island's vertical cliffs were a spectacle: no wonder the early explorers headed for this place. The dark folds of the mantle of curving rock are so splendidly displayed toward the sea that the sight fairly beckons one in, and the blue of the farther and green of the nearer hills make a perfect setting for the mysterious proud crest of Cadillac, the queen of the Maine shore.

Visibility was nearly unlimited. We could see the twin humps of the two islands (Little Duck and Great Duck) north of Lunts Harbor shortly after we came past Schoodic. We were going for Frenchboro, inside Lunts. We went straight on; the surge gave just enough of a swoop and rise to make things interesting.

We turned into the beautiful little cut of Lunts Harbor just in time to catch the slanting rays of the sun on the face of the church at the far end. We had made it over a rolling sea in just over two hours, averaging well over fourteen knots including slowdowns and such. There is no doubt that we had a cruising speed of sixteen knots. We were still on the spark plugs I had put in at Camden on August 18, just two weeks ago.

As we came to the float I saw what I thought was a woman tending gas dock, but no, it was an escaped Beatle. Maine's coast and New York City have this much in common: if a man wants to wear his hair long, well, that's his business.

A chunky barrel of a lobster fisherman was picking specimens out of the lobster car. I asked him why, if he fished lobster, he was buying. Well, he hadn't been out today and he just felt like having lobster, so he was buying some.

We were offered a mooring off the gas dock, accepted same gratefully, and settled down to make dinner. I was determined to have a new treat, "gin and conkles," that very night: I heated up a couple of inches of water in the saucepan and laid the conkles in. While they steamed, I drank gin and tomato juice and waited expectantly. At the end of thirty-five minutes, I was able to pry a conkle limp out of his shell using a fork, just like the old lobsterman said; I pulled off the tail section, removed the hard nose, and squeezed lemon juice over the fat little black-speckled thing, salted it well, and presto! the world's most far-out hors d'oeuvre. They were chewy and tasty and infinitely superior to cocktail dip.

Pat tried one and said that it was fine but she'd leave the rest to me. She will never be a Compleat Seafood Eater.

For an entree, after nineteen conkles, I had Pat's

*Criehaven harbor on Ragged Island,*
*sister to Matinicus Island*

*Coming into Matinicus Harbor*

charcoal-grilled pork chops (an hour in the making), apple sauce, zucchini, and lettuce and tomato salad. I told Pat I'd have just a small breakfast in the morning, I thought, with no bacon.

We sat and listened to the low boom of surf off the bar at the harbor entrance; we watched the antics of a young gull we could recognize by the frazzled feathers at the back of his head; this gull insisted on using our yacht for landings and takeoffs. We called him Pork Chop because he'd made a couple of tentative passes at dinner as it lay waiting on the fantail. I had fended him off with threatening gestures of my dinner fork. Now, with the dinner cleared, Pork Chop stood sadly on the forward deck, peering at us through the windshield, occasionally tapping softly with his beak or else just standing there shaking his head quickly back and forth every now and then as if to express disbelief at his cruel treatment.

The harbor is V-shaped; fishing houses line both steep shores one above the other and at the apex of the V sits the church. The trees come down to the shore between the houses which sit one above the other on the shelving hillsides; the compact but deep anchorage, the church, the houses, and the steep sides make Frenchboro unbeatable.

The town was once a sort of offshore pleasure dome for the fishing fleet, it has been said. Wild times ashore with wilder women. But no more. It is a sedate town and all the males are local fishermen.

Naturally, since it is only about ten miles from Mount Desert, Lunts Harbor is a great favorite with the yachtsmen of that many-yachted island. As we sat digesting dinner, a big black-hulled Hinckley, *Jack Tar,* out of Mount Desert was helmed in by a slim and active lady in a big, floppy, fashionable (I am sure) sun hat. She motored up to ask us if there were any moorings and I said she'd have to ask at the gas dock.

"I think I'll just take one out here and see what hap-

pens," she said briskly and steered the hull around to a mooring. There the *Jack Tar* swung and her two-man crew broiled steaks in a huge charcoal pot astern. The elegant lady then dinghied in and with her friends disappeared up the road; they came back late at night. Maybe there is life in the old town yet.

*Thursday, September 1.* We breakfasted to a good-morning visit by Pork Chop who was still clacking his beak and shaking his head. Today was to be a run to Matinicus since the Frenchboro–Matinicus–Monhegan route is most direct to Portland. We charged out of Lunts Harbor and set the course south of Isle au Haut, pushed *Puff's* throttles to full cruising and settled down for the thirty-mile run. This was real open ocean running. The seas lifted and sank under us, rolling huge swells in from the Azores and the land of Henry the Navigator. We began to treasure the little land we had left in our circle of vision. Outside Isle au Haut we got into a stiffer chop and had to come down to three-quarter speed; but the sea smoothed as we began to come within sight of Seal Island and then Wooden Ball Island, and we came back to top speed for the last third of the run, slipping between Matinicus and its sister island, Ragged Island, and making a left turn into the small harbor of Criehaven on Ragged first, arriving at 2:20, just two hours and one minute after leaving Lunts Harbor. (See Map Sixteen, page 214.)

The surge in the harbor was something fierce as we tied to the dock on the right. We had to rig spring lines fore and aft to keep the yacht from harm.

One of the island's lobster fishermen and a helper were mending pots; I needed a good sit in the sun and a leg stretch after the trip and we wanted fresh water for laundry. He kindly offered to send one of his sons up with our biggest water jug. We got into conversation about lobster rustlers. He said he'd caught one man. "Only had trouble with one fellow," said the fisherman.

*Matinicus herring dories*

*Matinicus town is built on stilts*
*in part, on granite in part*

"He started hauling my traps. Someone who was with him came and told me. I tried to do it legal. I went to the Game and Fisheries people and they said there was nothing they could do for me without *two* witnesses, so then I came back and went up to this fellow and I said, 'You been hauling my gear.' Then—I ain't ashamed to admit it—I did just what I always said I would. I hit him in the head and I told him to get off the island. He moved inside of a week. Nothing worse you can do to a man than haul his gear. I'd just as soon give him money out of my pocket."

My conversationalist was a top lobster fisherman, putting out five hundred traps. Every year he replaces a hundred that get lost, smashed, cut adrift by boats, or just plain give out. "You take oak," he said, "and you're lucky if you can nail together three in a day and knit the headers if you start from scratch. Now by the time you buy the line, each one of them is a ten-dollar bill." He held up a small plastic float. "Thirty-nine cents each," he said, "just to keep the line off the bottom."

He was also a man of parts. He had imported rabbits to Ragged for rabbit hunting. And he was raising pheasant and had a pen with 140 out in the back of the wharf. He let them go from time to time and they took to the wilds. "Some days when it blows, and we can't go out fishing, we go out and hunt pheasant. Shoot one and have him for dinner. They get real wild here. You aren't going to get every one you shoot at."

He also raised white duck We had noticed an abnormally tame breed of eider duck paddling about the harbor. It seemed that one of the fisherman's female white ducks had no luck hatching a clutch of eggs of her own and so he got her a bunch of eider duck eggs and she raised the brood which now swam happily and unafraid around the harbor.

There was an interruption when Pat and I saw one of the eider swimming on its back. It had lost its sense of balance and couldn't stay upright, trying frantically, but failing, to swim. Instead it did barrel rolls and piteous wiggles. Our friend sent one of his boys down to get it. When the boy brought it back our friend pinched the duck's breastbone. "Thin as a knife," he said. "Feed him some duck pellets, but put them in water because he can't eat without water. Must be a stray in here," he said.

I asked him how many of the lobster fishermen were out today. "Four," he said. "There's one, two, three, four, five boats left in the harbor."

I told him I thought he'd said previously that there were only eight fishing out of the harbor. He stopped, eyed me appraisingly, and with an expression of approval said, "Well, you got to have the whole story. This fellow, the ninth one, has money. He only puts out forty traps. He's only playing. I don't call him a fisherman.

"Now there's lobster fishermen who been at it all their lives and don't get lobster, or may get a few, but to really get lobster, you got to move with them. They come in, and they move out. Might only be a berth off, but they move. You just have to see how they move by what's in the traps. I keep some spotter traps going in deeper water, keep checking them once a week even though there's nothing in them. But I start catching them when they start going deeper and then I move

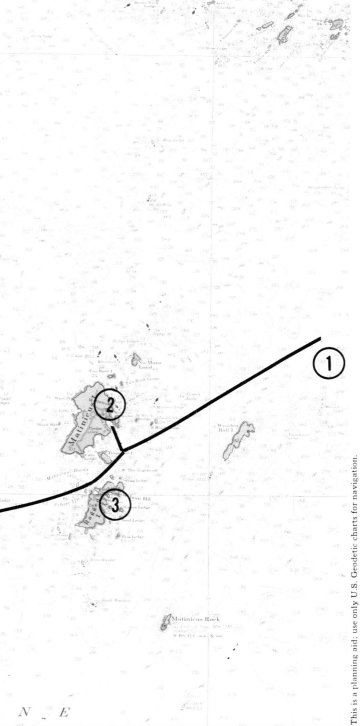

*Map 16: Return Course from Isle au Haut
to Monhegan Island*

1. SLIDE return course from Lunts Harbor, Long Island,
   going south of Isle au Haut and Wooden Ball Island.

2. Matinicus Harbor, Matinicus Island. The most strange
   and wondrous of all Maine's harbors.

3. Criehaven Harbor, Ragged Island. A small lobstering
   harbor and the farthest offshore, inhabited land
   on the Maine coast.

4. Monhegan Island. The famous, much-visited tourist
   and fishing island.

*N*  *E*

*Matinicus fishermen
straighten their net*

more of my traps out deep."

By now our water jug was back and we got down into *Puff,* hanging on her spring lines. Our friend warned us to hold onto our stern line because the surge was moving in toward the rocks at the end of the wharf and then out again, and he was afraid we'd get taken onto the rocks. I hung onto the stern line and used it as a pivot while Pat put the helm hard over and got us around and headed out.

We debated going to Monhegan for the night, which would have cut our final day's run by twenty miles; there was a report of a hurricane going off into the Atlantic from the Caribbean, so there would be bigger and heftier seas fairly soon, even though the big blow would pass many hundreds of miles off. Since Monhegan's harbor has only sketchy protection, we opted for our final night on Matinicus, the inside of these two islands. Matinicus is a salty place, as fine a valedictory port as you can choose.

We came into Matinicus harbor after twenty minutes just in time to see a herring boat crew running their net through a roller on a raft to get it straightened around. And lobster fishermen were coming in with their catch; in another place a nest of rafted herring dories rode at anchor. Beyond the harbor at Matinicus there is nothing but sea. It's far enough offshore so that you really feel that here is an *island*.

We tied up to the float and went ashore to see about taking some pictures—and this is postcard country. But the herring boat had come in to the float after us. I heard a voice say, "Get that damn thing out of the way!" I told Pat, "I think that's us." By the time we'd gotten back, the crew had tied our stern line to their stern to get it out of the way so they could lie. "I apologize," I said; "I am sorry we were in your way."

"It's all right," said the captain of the herring boat. He was an older, sharp-witted fellow with hair smoothed back and a certain authoritative command.

"You might have lost a couple of engines, that's all."

I asked him if there was a mooring to be had. Matinicus harbor was, as usual, close-packed with boats behind its granite breakwater. "Tie up alongside of one of the dories out there," said the man. "They're all mine. Pick any one."

So we did. *Puff* spent her last night on the cruise rafted with herring dories, those rowing hulls of elegant elemental form, an archetype of all sea craft. A fitting last port, indeed.

Matinicus town is reminiscent of Amalfi—or any small fishing village piled up on a coastal cliff over a harbor—there are gangways, planks over the rocks between houses, houses almost on top of other houses, a great deal of communal feeling and neighborly gatherings ashore, all very Old World.

*Friday, September 2.* Toward morning, I was awakened by the thud of our hull striking another. It was evident we were banging the dory. That was my first thought. My second was, "My God, it's rolling like crazy. The hurricane must have turned." I yanked open the snaps of the cockpit curtains and without bothering to dress, I scrambled out on deck, bare as God made me.

The situation over the side wasn't as bad as it had felt, by any means. There was a pronounced surge in the harbor but the skies were clear. The moon was full to her brim and casting a couple of million candlepower on the scene. But the dory and our yacht were definitely hitting. I saw that I would have to lengthen the bow line and shorten the stern line, so I leaped into the rocking dory and tried to untie the bow line. The line had knit itself into a tight knot. I couldn't get the strain off it long enough to get it untied; both boats were rocking and banging at a great rate; in the breeze my skin began to chill like the outside of a highball glass.

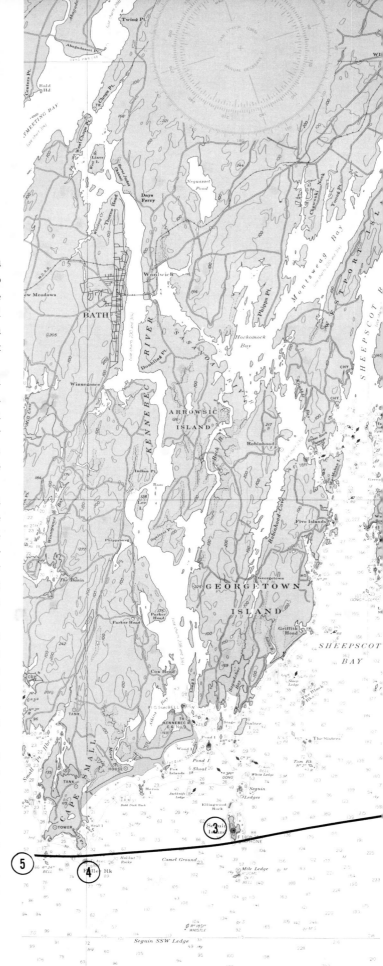

Once a cruise—at least—comes a moment when you suddenly wonder what crazy notion ever led you to go cruising. The moment when I was trying to hold the boats apart with one hand, trying to untie a rock-hard slippery-wet bow line with the other, pitching about in an old dory twenty miles from the mainland, stark naked in the moonlight, was definitely one of these.

I finally—before pneumonia could set in—wrestled the knot loose and performed the necessary operations. Once inside, of course, I spent forty minutes lying on my back looking up, wondering if the hurricane *really* had turned and, if so, where would I go for maximum protection and did I have enough insurance on the hull? Then I fell asleep.

Morning proved kinder than the night. It was a cloudless morning; there was not much wind and the roll hadn't built up, it had moderated. The **WEZE** weather broadcast said that Hurricane Faith had definitely gone out to sea and her powers were greatly diminished. There would be big swells later on but nothing that a yacht like *Puff TMD* couldn't handle gracefully.

Had things been otherwise, had Faith come up the coast toward Hatteras, we would have had a day to find some landlocked cove on the mainland to double anchor and wait it out. That is to say, we would have headed for shore immediately, at six in the morning. We would have gone without the leisurely breakfast that we did in fact enjoy.

Since the wind was moderate, I was confident we could make the seventy-odd miles to Falmouth Foreside by suppertime. With luck we could make it a good deal faster. There'd be no problem about having the boat picked up by Albert Frost since the company leases a couple of moorings at the Handy Boat Service. And the Handy is a nice place to finish off a cruise.

We came out of Matinicus harbor onto sizable mid-ocean-type swells. The effect of the swell meeting the

Map 17: Return Course from Monhegan to Casco Bay

1. SLIDE *return course coming from Monhegan Island.*

2. *Bantam Rock.*

3. *Seguin Island off the Kennebec River mouth.*

4. *Fuller Rock at the entrance to Casco Bay.*

5. SLIDE *return course to Falmouth Foreside, Portland, and Kittery.*

This is a planning aid: use only U.S. Geodetic charts for navigation.

reefs off Matinicus was spectacular. The sea was throwing skyward the most marvelous geysers, plumes, and minor atomic clouds of heavy white spume we'd seen on the cruise. (See Map Seventeen, page 221.)

We nipped between Matinicus and Ragged, had our last backward look at little Criehaven, and were off. Visibility was about six miles and we were soon all alone on the ocean, going for a mark off Monhegan Island somewhere out of sight. It was a good facsimile of being in mid-Atlantic. Hurricane Faith had generated sufficiently dramatic swells to complete the illusion. *Puff* worked hard going uphill and ran like a hydroplane downhill. Happily our twin forties were just getting properly broken in. We were doing seventeen and some and a rooster tail spun out behind us in a low long arc, testifying to the well-being of all the cylinders and working parts.

We soon began to pick up small blue smudges of islands to the west, and an occasional identifiable ledge, giving out white splendiferous fireworks that glinted piercingly in the morning sun, told us we were heading properly. We soon had Seal Island to the south and then the higher coast of Monhegan began to separate from the sea haze, dead on.

We came tearing by Monhegan's seaward shore. Its huge torn cliffs stood like a bastion against the leaping white floods thundering out of the edge of the sea; the seas scaled halfway to the top of Monhegan's parapets before being repulsed in streaming cascades. The island, so high and large, must have seemed a fine place to the early fishermen: it was far enough off the coast to be safe from surprise attack from Indians, and large enough to hold as many acres of drying racks as needed for the catches brought back by ships bulging from their depredations on the fish that streamed by the shores in seemingly inexhaustible supply. The first fishery set up here was by John Smith when the 1600s were only a few years old.

As we went by the lower rocks of the southeastern tip and could look up into the open-ended harbor, we spotted a painting class, presumably doing their best to capture the essence of the high flung spray. I wondered if *Puff*, a white sea moth with glittering, beating wings of spray jetting out, would be caught memorably by the palette of some future Winslow Homer.

I was now sad that we had to miss Monhegan. It is an island of many charming nooks, of art, of long habitation by an independent folk. It is the piece of land most constantly inhabited on the coast, and has the assured air of a place that will continue to be, even if the mainland is abandoned.

From Monhegan, it is a straight shoot, almost without marks, to the ledges on the far side of Penobscot Bay and then to Sequin Light off the Kennebec.

Again we were alone at sea. *Puff*, seeming to sense that this was homestretch work, disdainfully spat aside the small chop rising on the swells. With only a small crackling comment, she roared up and drove readily down the sides of the huge mementos of Hurricane Faith.

We now ticked off the island of Seguin and its high round light and went for the spray-soaked beacon on Fuller Rock at the opening of Casco Bay. We were headed into the world of civilized islands. And so into

*Finis at Handy's, Casco Bay.*

*Have dinghy, will travel*

Casco Bay, running past Ragged Island, where Edna St. Vincent Millay wrote, past the Eagle Island of Admiral Peary and past our landfall on Cliff Island, and into the inner ranks of islands guarding the mainland at Falmouth Foreside.

The wide-open spaces of the Maine coast began to narrow: we met more power cruisers in the next hour than we had met in the whole preceding four weeks.

I wanted to get up on the cabin top and shout "Go East!" because here were swarms of power boats buzzing in Casco Bay like a cloud of claustrophilic bees while outside great things awaited—innumerable Thrumcaps, Roaring Bulls, Thumpers, and other mythological beasts, all spouting fountains of wrath; also waiting were the zestful rollers of Hurricane Faith and the thousands of Maine's inimitable coastal land bits and ledges; there were harbors with tales to tell, basins with tide falls, long, intricate passages and tide rips and other wonders too thick to enumerate.

I imagined Champlain, John Smith, Verrazano: how impatiently they loaded their reports with glowing adjectives, trying to goad the homebodies into adventure. They could not understand how any man who called himself a sailor could putter about the tame shores of the Continent. Across the sea there was a whole new raw exciting bonanza waiting to be explored and exploited.

*Puff* rounded the final turn and the final marks off Clapboard Island now. The Portland Yacht Club moorings and the adjacent nautical hive of Handy Boat Service appeared.

We luckily found float space right away at the Handy. Boats were coming in and leaving as fast as shoppers through the glass doors of Macy's. We tied up by two o'clock, a fast four-and-a-half-hour run from Matinicus. The compactness of the coast here is a continuous surprise and advantage. We had been two-thirds of the way up the whole coast, sampled the best

that is to be found on it, and yet we had no trouble coming back in three days of relatively easy running.

And now the awful task of off-loading. By the time we'd disgorged the entire cargo, the float was listing heavily to our side. The mound of material looked sufficient to sustain a small party of Mount Everest climbers for a well-thought-out three-month assault. We worked slowly and the pile grew, and yachts were hesitating to approach the float, thinking that they must be interfering with the preparations for a new Northwest Passage attempt.

After this, we wasted little time in going up the gangplank to shower and change clothes, before coming back to the boat for a ceremonial drink.

*Enfin,* much water under the keel, much gin over it. 'Ere's to hull that bore us without fault and the engines that took us so far without complaint. 'Ere's to Bendix, Danforth, Samson, and Raytheon, to the Geodetic Survey, and 'ere's to the Coast Guard what puts out all the marks. 'Ere's to the ledges we missed and the landfalls made, and finally 'ere's to us wot made the bloody trip.

I, somewhat light-headed, took a lightened *Puff* out to a mooring which was lent us; I resisted the temptation to run her although I was sure she'd go well over twenty, light as she was. I tied her and left her floating there, keeping the jaunty cut of her bow in my eye as I rowed *X-ray* back to the float. Pat had meanwhile gotten hold of two carts from Handy and had started to load the gear. A whole flock of yachtsmen were soon down on the float, lending a hand. The eight hundred pounds or so was up on the parking lot in a matter of minutes. We had just piled the last gear (including *X-ray*) in the lot as my brother Jon came driving up with my VW bus. As he stepped from the car, Jon said, "The caption for this scene is 'Have dinghy, will travel.'"

Have dinghy and have traveled. It was over, all but telling the stories.

PHOTO CREDITS

*All photographs by the author except for the following:*

*page 18: George Daniell*

*page 28: Maine Department of Economic Development*

*page 35: Maine Department of Sea and Shore Fisheries*

*page 41: National Fisherman*

*page 42: National Fisherman*

*page 45: Maine Department of Economic Development*

*page 47: Maine Department of Economic Development*

*page 48: Maine Department of Economic Development*

*page 50: Maine Department of Economic Development*

*page 53: Maine Department of Economic Development*

*page 54: Timothy Adams*

*page 65: Maine Department of Sea and Shore Fisheries*

*page 106: Kim Massie*

*page 118: Kim Massie*

*page 119: Kim Massie*

*page 124: Maine Department of Economic Development*

*page 144: W. H. Ballard*

*page 159: National Fisherman*

*page 172: W. H. Ballard*

*page 177: F. B. Shattuck*

*page 179: National Fisherman*

*page 222: Jon Lund*

*page 223: Jon Lund*

*Book designed by Form 3, Inc.*